A SIMPLIFIED GRAMMAR OF THE
JAPANESE LANGUAGE

THE UNIVERSITY OF CHICAGO PRESS
CHICAGO, ILLINOIS

✳

THE BAKER & TAYLOR COMPANY
NEW YORK

THE CAMBRIDGE UNIVERSITY PRESS
LONDON

A SIMPLIFIED GRAMMAR *of* *the* JAPANESE LANGUAGE

(*Modern written style*)

By

BASIL HALL CHAMBERLAIN

REVISED EDITION BY

COLONEL JAMES GARFIELD McILROY

United States Army

THE UNIVERSITY OF CHICAGO PRESS

CHICAGO · ILLINOIS

PREFACE

This is a grammar of the modern Japanese written language. It is a revision of the *Simplified Japanese Grammar* by Basil Hall Chamberlain, published in 1881, and now out of print. During the several years in which I studied Japanese, Chamberlain's book was the only one which gave me any clear idea of the written language. After a thorough study of his work I saw where it could be enlarged and improved so as to be of much more value to the student of today. In this revision, my constant aim has been simplicity and practicability.

The most important variation from the original edition is the use of the general rule by which the written verb can be quickly separated into its stem and its inflection (§ 266). Based on this rule an alphabetically arranged list of verb and adjective inflections of the Japanese written language is given in this edition for reference (p. 113). The addition of this list and the index of Japanese words and phrases will make this book a grammatical dictionary for the student's or translator's desk.

The student or translator should at once make himself thoroughly familiar with chapter xi, so that the inflected list can be used without delay.

A debt of gratitude is due Mr. Chamberlain for permitting the unqualified use and modification of his excellent work. Also, I wish here to express my appreciation of the many helpful suggestions received from Messrs. Edwin L. Neville, Renkei Tsuda, and W. Koseki.

J. G. McIlroy

CONTENTS

[vii]

CONTENTS

INTRODUCTION

THE JAPANESE LANGUAGE

In Japan, as in other Eastern countries, two dialects are used simultaneously, one for speaking, the other for writing. The spoken or colloquial dialect is that to which foreign-government officials, merchants, missionaries, and others who are brought into daily relations with the Japanese must devote their first efforts. Their next step should be to acquire the written language, without a knowledge of which practically all books, newspapers, postcards, advertisements, railway-station placards, or steamship notices remain a mystery, even when transliterated into Roman characters. Some of the differences affect the vocabulary. But the constantly recurring difficulties are rather in the grammar, and may be mastered in a comparatively short time by those to whom the colloquial is familiar.

Heretofore, the great obstacle has been the absence of any book specially devoted to the elucidation of the modern form of the written language. Most persons have neither time nor inclination to investigate the Japanese classics or to carry on philological research. Their concern is with the language as commonly written now; and they weary of searching through the pages of a learned work for the everyday forms, which alone to them are useful. The object of the present book is to put before such persons, in as simple and practicable a manner as possible, just so much as will enable them to read contemporary literature. All forms that are obsolete or purely classical have been omitted. Theoretical discussions have been dispensed with, save in a few instances where a knowledge of theory is, for a foreigner, the only road to correct practice.

Japanese literature has flourished without interruption since the eighth century. One consequence of this long and varied career of the Japanese language is the existence at the present day of a number of styles distinguished by strongly marked peculiarities. Leaving aside poetry and a certain ornamental kind of prose cultivated chiefly by a few Shinto scholars, there are four categories of style in common use.

I. The semi-classical style, distinguished by its preference for old native words and grammatical forms. (The standard translation of the New Testament is in this style.)

II. The semi-colloquial style, used much in newspapers. Its phraseology savors largely, and its grammar slightly, of the peculiarities of the modern colloquial dialect.

III. The Chinese style, or Sinico-Japanese, which is replete with Chinese words and idioms. It is founded on the literal translations of the Chinese classics, which were formerly the text-books in every school. This style is used in the higher type of contemporary literature. We find it in technical books, in some magazines, and in editorials of newspapers.

IV. The epistolary style. Almost exclusively Chinese in phraseology, this style has grammatical peculiarities which are so marked as to necessitate treatment in a separate chapter. It is in general use for all correspondence.

NECESSITY FOR A GRAMMAR IN "ROMAJI"

The system of writing that is in use in Japan is an extremely complicated one, semi-ideographic and semi-syllabic. The ideographs or characters, so called, have been borrowed from Chinese. The syllabary or **kana,** as it is called in Japanese, is a group of Chinese characters which have been abbreviated and are used phonetically by the Japanese. Uninflected words are written in characters only. Inflected words, that is, the verb and adjective, are written with one or more characters, followed by one or more **kana.** These **kana** are used for the purpose of denoting the inflections, but as a matter of fact they do not convey a clear idea of the structure of the Japanese verb or adjective. In almost every case the true stem ends in a consonant which the Japanese language, as written, has no means of showing. The foreign student consequently is frequently confused in attempting to understand the innumerable inflected forms of Japanese verbs and adjectives as they appear in the literature of Japan today.

But the language may be written in Roman characters, and when so written the stems and inflections of the verbs and adjectives show up clearly. What appeared so difficult and confusing to the student becomes then comparatively simple. A purely phonetic system of transliteration has been adopted, and has met with some acceptance both among Japanese and foreigners. To this system the spelling of the following pages conforms.

PARTS OF SPEECH

The words of which the Japanese language is composed fall into two great groups, the uninflected and the inflected.

The uninflected words are: (*a*) the *noun*, which, besides the substantive properly so called, includes the *pronoun*, the *numeral*, and many words corresponding to English adjectives; (*b*) the *particle;* and (*c*) the *postposition*, corresponding for the most part to the English particle and preposition. The inflected words are: (*a*) the *adjective;* (*b*) the *verb* (including participles). This division is not an artificial one made for the sake of convenience, but has its foundation in the nature and history of the language.

What we term *adverbs* in English are replaced partly by nouns, partly by one of the inflections of the adjective. *Conjunctions* are largely included under the heading of particles and postpositions, but also often expressed by certain inflections of the verb. *Interjections* exist, as in other languages; but, being mere isolated words without grammatical connection with the sentence, they call for no remark. The Japanese language has no *article*.

From one part of speech another may often be formed by adding certain terminations. Thus: **rashiki** serves to form adjectives expressive of similarity, while more rarely **nau** forms verbs expressive of action, as: **otoko,** "man"; **otokorashiki,** "manly." **tomo,** "company"; **tomonau,** "to accompany."

CHAPTER I

THE PHONETIC SYSTEM

ALPHABET AND PRONUNCIATION

1. Japanese, when written with the Roman alphabet, requires the same letters as English, with the exception of *l, q, v,* and *x.* The letter **c** occurs only in the combination **ch,** which is sounded nearly like English *ch* in "church."

2. The vowels are sounded as in Italian: **a** as in "father"; **i** as in "pique"; **u** as in "rude"; **e** as in "prey"; **o** as in "home." They are always short unless marked with the sign of long quantity, when care must be taken to pronounce them long, thus: **do,** "a degree"; **dō,** "a hall." **toru,** "to take"; **tōru,** "to pass through." **kuki,** "a stem"; **kūki,** "the air."

The only long vowels of common occurrence are **ō** and **ū.** They are found chiefly in words of Chinese origin, where they represent such Chinese diphthongs and nasal sounds as **ao, ou, ang, ung,** etc.

When preceded by another vowel or by **n, e** sounds very nearly like **ye,** i like **yi,** and o like **wo.** Thus **ue, kon-in,** and **shio** are respectively pronounced **uye, kon-yin,** and **shiwo.**

The vowels i and u are sometimes inaudible, or nearly so, in the mouths of Tokyo speakers, as **shite,** "having done," pronounced **shte; jinrikisha,** pronounced **jinriksha; tsuki,** "the moon," pronounced **tski; takusan,** "much," pronounced **taxan; watakushi,** "I," pronounced **watakshi.** Initial **u** is silent, and the following **m** doubled in the pronunciation of the four words **uma,** "horse"; **umaki,** "tasty"; **umaruru,** "to be born"; **ume,** "plum tree," pronounced **mma, mmaki, mmaruru, mme.** But these deviations are slight and unimportant. All the foregoing words will be understood if pronounced as written.

3. The diphthongs, such as **ao, au, ei, ii, ou,** call for no special comment, as each vowel retains its own proper sound.

4. The consonants are pronounced approximately as in English, subject to the following remarks:

f is a true labial. In pronouncing this letter the under lip does not touch the upper teeth but only approaches them, the result being like a strongly aspirated *wh*.

g never has the sound of **j**. At the beginning of a word it is pronounced hard, like the *g* in *give*. In the middle of a word it has the sound of English *ng* in "longing." Thus **Kiga**, the name of a place, rhymes almost exactly with "singer" ("singa"), as pronounced in the southeastern portion of the United States (not with "finger"). The words **ga,** "of," and **gotoki,** "like," also take the *ng* sound.

h before **i** sounds nearly like the German *ch* in "mich," and sometimes passes almost into *sh*.

n at the end of a word is pronounced halfway between a true *n* and the French nasal *n*. Nouns having a final **n** are mostly of Chinese origin.

y is always a consonant. Thus the syllable **mya** in **myaku,** "the pulse," is pronounced as one syllable, like *mia* in the English word "amiable." Care must be taken not to confound it with the dissyllable in such words as **miyako,** "a capital city."

z has almost the sound of **dz** when preceding the vowel **u;** thus **mizu,** "water," is pronounced almost **midzu**.

Double consonants must be distinctly sounded, as in Italian, thus: **kite,** "having come"; **kitte,** "a ticket." **koka,** "an ancient poem"; **kokka,** "hearth and home."

5. Generally speaking, the Japanese pronunciation both of vowels and of consonants is less broad and heavy than that current in most European languages, and especially in English. This applies more particularly to the letters **ch, j, r, sh,** and **ts.** Tones, such as those of the Chinese, are entirely absent. There is little or no tonic accent, and only a very slight rhetorical

[5]

accent; that is to say, that all the syllables of a word and all the words of a sentence are pronounced equally, or nearly so. Students must beware of importing into Japanese the strong and constantly recurring stress by which we in English single out one syllable in every word, and the chief words in every sentence.

5. All Japanese words end either in a vowel or in the consonant **n.** There are no combinations of consonants excepting **ts** and the double consonants already mentioned, among which must be counted **ssh** and **tch,** standing for double **sh** and double **ch,** as in **kesshin,** "resolve"; **zetchō,** "peak." By some very careful speakers **w** is pronounced after **k** in many words taken from the Chinese. Thus **kwannin,** "an official"; **Gwaimushō,** "the Foreign Office." But the pronunciation current in Tokyo and in most parts of the country is simply **kannin, Gaimushō.**

LETTER-CHANGES

7. "**Nigori,**" i.e., "muddling," is the name given by the Japanese to the substitution of sonants for surds.[1]

8. The consonants affected are:

ch
sh } which change into **j**

f
h } which change into **b**

k   which changes into **g**

s
ts } which change into **z**

t   which changes into **d**

NOTE.—**F** and **h** also often change into **p,** especially in Chinese compounds. This is called "**han-nigori,**" i.e., "half-muddling."

9. The rule regarding the **nigori,** stated broadly, is that the initial surd of an independent word changes into the correspond-

---

[1] In contradistinction to the sonant letters, the surd letters are said to be **sumi,** i.e., "clear." The two categories together are termed **sei-daku, sei** being the Chinese equivalent for "clear," and **daku** for "muddled."

ing sonant when the word is used as the second member of a compound, thus:

kuni-ju, "throughout the land," from kuni and chū
waru-jare, "a practical joke," from waruki and share
fune-bune, "all sorts of vessels," from fune repeated
mushiba, "a decayed tooth," from mushi and ha
hongoku, "native country," from hon and koku
ronzuru, "to discuss," from ron and suru
kanzume, "tinned," from kan and tsume
kondate, "a bill of fare," from kon and tate

The foregoing rule is by no means an absolute one, euphony, and sometimes the varying caprice of individuals, deciding in each case whether the change shall or shall not take place. F and h, however, always change either into b or into p if the first member of the compound ends in the consonant n, thus:

nampū, "the south wind," from nan and fū
sam-ben, "three times," from san and hen

10. As shown in the preceding examples, n changes into m before a labial.

11. The following category of changes affects a large number of compound words of Chinese origin, and notably the numerals as combined with the "auxiliary numerals" (§§ 47, 48):

ch it-chō for ichi-chō "one"
hat-chō for hachi chō "eight"
jit-chō for jū chō "ten"

f and h ip-puku for ichi-fuku ⎫
ip-piki for ichi hiki ⎬ "one"

sam-buku for san fuku ⎫
sam-biki for san hiki ⎬ "three"

rop-puku for roku fuku ⎫
rop-piki for roku hiki ⎬ "six"

jip-puku for jū fuku ⎫
jip-piki for jū hiki ⎬ "ten"

hyap-puku for hyaku fuku ⎫ "hundred"
hyap-piki for hyaku hiki ⎭

sem-buku for sen fuku ⎫ "thousand"
sem-biki for sen hiki ⎭

k ik-ken for ichi ken "one"
san-gen for san ken "three"
rok-ken for roku ken "six"
jik-ken for jū ken "ten"
hyak-ken for hyaku ken "hundred"
sen-gen for sen ken "thousand"

m sam-mai for san-mai "three"
sem-mai for sen mai "thousand"

s is-sō for ichi sō "one"
sanzō for san sō "three"
has-sō for hachi sō "eight"
jis-sō for ju sō "ten"
sen-zō for sen sō "thousand"

sh is-shu for ichi shu "one"
has-shu for hachi shu "eight"
jis-shu for jū shu "ten"

t it-tsū for ichi tsū "one"
hat-tsū for hachi tsū "eight"
jit-tsū for jū tsū "ten"

Similarly, as-sei for atsu sei "tyranny"
hak-kō for hatsu kō "issuing"
kessuru for ketsu suru "to resolve"

w sam-ba for san wa "three"
rop-pa for roku wa "six"
jip-pa for ju wa "ten"

12. The Japanese cannot pronounce all their consonants before all their vowels. This leads to the following euphonic laws:

a) **d, j,** and **z** are correlated in such wise that **d** stands only before the three vowels, **a, e,** and **o; j** only before **a, i, o,** and **u;**

and **z** only before **a, e, o, u.** Apparent irregularities are hereby caused in the conjugation of many verbs, thus:

INDEFINITE FORM	ATTRIBUTIVE PRESENT
ide	**izuru,** "to go forth"
ōji	**ōzuru,** "to correspond"

b) **f** and **h** are similarly correlated, **f** standing only before **u,** and **h** only before the other four vowels, thus:

INDEFINITE FORM	ATTRIBUTIVE PRESENT
he	**furu,** "to pass"

c) **s** and **sh** are correlated, **sh** standing only before **i,** and **s** only before the other four vowels, thus:

INDEFINITE FORM	ATTRIBUTIVE PRESENT
kashi	**kasu,** "to lend"

d) **t, ts,** and **ch** are correlated, **t** standing only before **a, e,** and **o; ts** only before **u;** and **ch** only before **a, i, o,** and **u,** thus:

INDEFINITE	ATTRIBUTIVE	NEGATIVE	CAUSATIVE
tachi	**tatsu**	**tatazu**	**tatashimuru,** "to stand"

e) **w** is inserted before **a** in verbal terminations when another vowel precedes, thus:

INDEFINITE	ATTRIBUTIVE	NEGATIVE	CAUSATIVE
warai	**warau**	**warawazu**	**warawashimuru,** "to laugh"

f) **y** disappears before **e** and **i,** thus:

kie	**kiyuru,** "to melt"

13. A few monosyllables and dissyllables of pure native origin ending in **e** change the **e** into **a** when used as the first member of a compound, thus:

kana-gu, "metal work," from **kane** and **gu.**
ta-makura, "the arm used as a pillow," from **te** and **makura.**
uwa-zutsumi, "an outer wrapper," from **ue** and **tsutsumi.**[1]

---

[1] In reality **kana, ta,** etc., are the original forms, which have become softened into **kane, te,** etc., except in compounds.

CHAPTER II

THE NOUN

THE SUBSTANTIVE PROPERLY SO CALLED

14. The substantive is indeclinable, distinctions of number and gender being left to be gathered from the context, and case relations being, as in English, indicated by independent words. Thus, the substantive **ushi** signifies "bull," "ox," "cow," "bulls," "oxen," "cows," "cattle," according to circumstances. The phrase **ushi wo kau** signifies "to keep cattle"; **ushi ni noru,** "to ride on a bull" if one rider is alluded to, and "to ride on bulls" if several persons are spoken of; **ushi wo kuu,** "to eat beef"; and **ushi no chichi,** "cow's milk."

15. In the extremely rare cases in which it is absolutely indispensable to mention the sex of an animal, this can be done by prefixing some independent word, such as **o,** "male"; **me,** "female." Thus: **o-ushi,** "a bull"; **me-ushi,** "a cow."

16. What we call the singular number is occasionally indicated by the use of the word **ichi** or **hitotsu,** "one." Thus: **ichi-nen,** "one year"; **tama hitotsu,** "one ball."

Plurality is occasionally indicated by doubling the word (the second half of the compound thus obtained usually taking the **"nigori"** [§§ 7–11]), thus: **hōbō,** "all sides," "everywhere," from **hō,** "side"; **kuni-guni,** "various countries," from **kuni,** "country." Or by prefixing or suffixing some word conveying the idea of number, thus: **ban-koku,** "all countries," "international," from **ban,** "myriad," and **koku,** "country"; **sho-kun,** "gentlemen," from **sho,** "all," and **kun,** "gentleman"; **su-nen,** "many years," from **sū,** "number," and **nen,** "year"; **onna-domo,** "women," from **onna,** "woman," and **tomo,** "companion." But such locutions are somewhat exceptional, distinctions of number not being dwelt upon at every turn by the Japanese as they are by the Aryan mind.

17. Compounds are very common, and can be formed at will. As in English, the first member of the compound generally defines the second, as will be seen by the numerous examples throughout this grammar. However, occasionally the two members are co-ordinated, as **kin-gin,** "gold and silver." This co-ordination sometimes (in imitation of Chinese idiom) assumes a peculiar form, which has been termed the "synthesis of contradictories," e.g., **chō-tan,** "long or short," i.e., "length"; **kan-dan,** "hot or cold," i.e., "temperature"; **nan-nyo,** "man or woman," i.e., "sex"; **yoshi-ashi,** "good or bad," i.e., "the moral character" of an action; **aru-nashi,** "there being or not being," i.e., "the question of the existence of a thing." Two contraries thus combined do duty for a single English abstract word, thus: **bun no ato-saki,** "the context (lit., the after-before) of a passage."

When one member of the compound is a verb governing the other, it comes second if the word is of Japanese origin, and first if it is of Chinese origin. Thus **funa-oroshi,** "a launch," "ship lowered"; **kami-hasami,** "hair-cutting" (Japanese); but **ki-kyō,** "returning to the capital"; **zō-sen,** "building a ship," "ship-building" (Chinese).

18. Hyphens are used in Romanized Japanese for the sake of clearness in very long compounds, and in those whose first member ends in **n** while the second commences with a vowel or with **y,** as **gen-an,** "the draft" of a document, not to be confounded with **genan,** "a common man." In the present work hyphens are used very freely to illustrate the sense and derivation of many words.

NOUNS USED AS ADJECTIVES AND ADVERBS

19. Japanese has comparatively few true adjectives, and in a great number of cases uses nouns instead, just as in English we say "a *gold* watch," "a *Turkey* carpet." A noun may do duty for an adjective in three ways:

a) As a member of a compound, thus: **Butsu-ji,** "Buddhist temple," from **Butsu,** "Buddha" or "Buddhism," and **ji,** "a temple"; **tei-koku,** "an imperial country," "an empire," from **tei,** "emperor," and **koku,** "country."

b) Followed by the postposition **no,** "of," thus: **gaikoku no kōsai,** "foreign intercourse," lit., "intercourse of foreign countries."

c) Followed by the attributive form of one of the tenses of the verb **naru,** "to be," thus: **kenso naru michi,** "a steep road," lit., "a steepness-being road"; **shinsetsu narishi hito,** "a kind person," lit., "kindness having-been person."

20. Words of this third class correspond to English adverbs, if the postposition **ni** (more rarely **to**) is substituted for the verb **naru,** thus: **kenso ni,** "steeply"; **shizen to,** "naturally."

21. Many words corresponding to English adverbs are formed by reduplicating nouns, as **tabi-tabi,** "often," from **tabi,** "a time." Many such reduplicated words are formed to produce the sound made by the thing signified. They are similar to the English "ding-dong," "pell-mell," etc.; thus **gasa-gasa** or **goso-goso,** representing a rustling sound; **tobo-tobo,** descriptive of the tottering steps of an old crone. Occasionally they are derived from adjective stems, as **sugo-sugo,** descriptive of low spirits, from **sugoki,** "ill at ease."

22. All Chinese words are treated as nouns by the Japanese, being used either as substantives proper, e.g., **kin,** "gold"; **jitsu,** "truth"; adjectively, according to one or other of the three methods mentioned in § 19; adverbially, by suffixing **ni** or **to,** e.g., **jitsu ni,** "truly"; as verbs, by suffixing **suru,** "to do," e.g., **kes-suru,** "to decide"; or as in § 21.

CHAPTER III

THE PRONOUN

PERSONAL PRONOUNS

23. The Japanese words corresponding to the personal pronouns of European languages are simply nouns whose original significations are in most cases perfectly clear, and which are indeed still often used with those significations. They answer to such English expressions as "your humble servant" (meaning "I"). Self-depreciatory terms are naturally used to represent what we should call the first person, and complimentary terms to represent the second person, thus:

boku, "servant"
shō-sei, "small born," "young"
soregashi, "a certain person"
ware (original meaning uncertain) } I
watakushi, "selfishness"
yo (etymology uncertain), etc.

Hei-ka, "beneath the steps of the throne"
(the idea being that a subject does not
dare to address the sovereign directly, } Your Majesty
but only prostrates his petition at the
Imperial Feet)

Kak-ka, "beneath the council-chamber"   Your Excellency

Ki-ka, "beneath augustness"
Kimi, "prince"
nanji (believed to have originally meant } You
"renowned")
sok-ka, "beneath the feet," etc.

NOTE.---Some of these are also used as titles suffixed to other nouns; thus: **Tennō Heika,** "His Majesty the Emperor."

24. Postpositions can be suffixed to the foregoing, as to any other nouns; thus: **soregashi no,** "of me," "my"; **soregashi wo,** "me." Instead of **ware no,** "of me," "my," the form **waga** (for **ware ga**) is in common use.

25. The plural suffixes are more often used with the quasi-personal pronouns than with any other class of nouns; thus: **ware-ra** (or **ware-ware**), **watakushi-domo** (sometimes also used for the singular), **yo-ra,** "we"; **kimi-tachi, sokka-tachi, nanji ra,** "you." In some cases plurality is otherwise expressed as by the term **waga hai,** lit., "our company," the usual equivalent for the English editorial "we."

26. The only word closely corresponding to our pronouns of the third person is **kare,** "that." Paraphrases, such as **kano hito,** "that person" (i.e., "he" or "she"), are sometimes employed, as are also the honorific designations mentioned above as equivalents for the second person. Very often the word **sono,** which properly means "that" (French *ce*), is used to signify "his," "her," "its"; thus: **sono haha,** "his mother."

27. The word **onore** (plural **onore-ra**), "self," may be of any person, but it is most commonly met with in the sense of "I."

28. The quasi-personal pronouns are very little used, the information they might supply being left to be gathered from the context in ninety-nine cases out of a hundred in which personal pronouns would be used by the speakers of European tongues.

REFLEXIVE PRONOUNS

29. The nouns corresponding to our reflexive pronouns are **jibun, jishin, onore,** "self"; **ono ga,** "own"; **waga,** properly "my," but also used more generally in the sense of "own," "one's own." They are comparatively little used.

DEMONSTRATIVE AND INTERROGATIVE PRONOUNS

30. The words answering to our demonstrative and interrogative pronouns are:

kore, "this" (Latin *hic*, French *celui-ci, celle-ci, ceci*)
sore, "that" (Latin *iste*, French *celui-là, celle-là, cela*)

kare, "that," "he," "she," "**it**" (Latin *ille,* French *celui-là, celle-là, cela*)
tare, "who?"
nani, "what?"
izure, "which?"

31. The foregoing are the substantive forms, before leaving which the student should note the plurals **kore-ra,** "these" (*ceux-ci, celles-ci*), **sore-ra** and **kare-ra** (*ceux-là, celles-là*).

32. The adjective forms, i.e., those that are employed to define nouns, are:

> **kono,** "this" (Latin *hic,* French *ce*)
> **sono,** "that" (Latin *iste,* French *ce*)
> **kono,** "that" (Latin *ille,* French *ce*)

33. The forms **kono, sono,** and **kano** also do duty for **kore no,** "of this"; **sore no** and **kare no,** "of that," of which they are contractions; thus **kono kuni,** "*this* country"; **kono tame ni,** "for the sake *of this.*" **Sono** also frequently means "his," "her," "its."

34. Tare is used of persons only, **nani** of things only (save in one or two compounds such as **nani-bito** or **nam-pito,** "what person?"), **izure** of both persons and things.

35. "What kind of?" is expressed by **ika naru,** the corresponding adverb **ika ni** meaning "how?"

36. Note also **itsu,** "when?" and **izuko,** "where?" words which are really nouns, though corresponding to English interrogative adverbs. Like other nouns, they take postpositions to modify their sense, thus:

> **itsu no koto narishi?** lit., "It was a thing of when?" i.e., "When did it happen"?
> **izuko ye,** lit., "to where?" i.e., "whither?"
> **izuko yori,** lit., "from where?" i.e., "whence?"
> **tare no,** "whose?"
> **nani no,** "what?"
> **izure no,** "which?"

INDEFINITE PRONOUNS

37. The indefinite pronouns are formed from **tare, nani,** and **izure** in the following manner:

> **tare mo,** "anyone," "everyone"; **tare ka,** "someone"
> **nani mo,** "anything," "everything"; **nani ka,** "something"
> **izure mo,** "either," "both," "all"; **izureka,** "one or other," "which"

RELATIVE PRONOUNS

38. The Japanese language has no relative pronouns or relative words of any kind. The way in which their absence is made good will be understood from the following examples: **yukishi hito,** "the person who went" (lit., "the went person"); **hisu-beki koto,** "a thing which should be kept secret" (lit., "a should-keep-secret thing").

39. As seen by these examples, the verb or adjective of the relative clause must be put in the attributive form. If there are several relative clauses, then only the verb or adjective of the last clause takes the attributive form, all the preceding clauses having the verb or adjective in the indefinite form.[1] Thus: **Kokorozashi tesseki wo idaki, gi wa sosetsu wo azamuki, fubo saishi wo mo on no tame ni enri shi, hisshi wo issen ni kiwameshi yūshi shi-jū-shichi nin,** "Forty-seven heroes, whose determination was as iron, whose devotion was not to be damped by difficulty, who for their lord's sake had left father and mother, wife and children, and who had resolved to sacrifice their lives in the attempt."

Here **idaki, azamuki,** and **shi** are the indefinite forms of the verbs **idaku, azamuku** (§ 138), and **suru** (§ 146), while **kiwameshi** is the attributive form of the first past tense of **kiwamuru** (§134*c*).

40. Occasionally the Japanese equivalents of English relative clauses appear ambiguous. Thus: **mishi hito,** lit., "the saw person," may signify either "the person who saw," or "the person

---

[1] For an explanation and illustrations of these very important technical terms see chap. vii and beginning of chap. viii.

whom I (you, he, etc.) saw"; **idasu tokoro,** lit., "the send place,"
may be either "the place *whence* something is sent," or "the place
to which something is sent." But a glance at the context generally leaves no doubt as to the meaning. For instance, **sa omoishi
wake** cannot mean "the reason which thought so," as such a
collocation of words would have no sense. It can only be inter-
preted to signify "the reason *for which* I (he, etc.), thought so."
Similarly, **shuttatsu seshi toki** can only mean "the time *when* I
(he, etc.) started." As seen by the foregoing examples, the
prepositions which often accompany an English relative pronoun
are not expressed in Japanese.[1]

41. Not infrequently the words **tokoro no** (more rarely **no**
alone) are inserted between the attributive and the noun, as
mishi tokoro no hito instead of the shorter **mishi hito,** "the man
I saw"; **sude ni nareru no nochi** for **sude ni nareru nochi,** "after
it had already been done." These circumlocutions add nothing
to the sense; their use originated in the imitation of Chinese
idiom. Sometimes, however, **no** legitimately represents the English relative, thus: **on hanashi no kenken,** "the various matters
which were mentioned by you" (lit., "the matter-matter of the
honorable speaking").

[1] Compare such English expressions as "dining-room," signifying "a room *in
which* people dine"; "shaving-brush," signifying "a brush *with which* you help
yourself to shave," etc.

CHAPTER IV

THE NUMERAL

THE CARDINAL NUMBERS

42. There are two sets of numerals, one of native and the other of Chinese origin. The native set is now obsolete except for the first ten numbers, which are as follows:

1. hitotsu	6. mutsu
2. futatsu	7. nanatsu
3. mitsu	8. yatsu
4. yotsu	9. kokonotsu
5. itsutsu	10. tō

43. These numerals may either be used as independent words, or compounded with substantives. When used independently, they may either stand quite alone, or follow or (very rarely) precede a substantive, or stand in an attributive relation to the substantive by means of the postposition **no;** thus: **futatsu ari,** "there are two"; **hako futatsu,** or **futatsu no hako,** "two boxes."

44. When compounded, they invariably precede the substantive. In this case the first nine drop the syllable **tsu,** which is properly a suffix, and long **tō** becomes short **to;** thus: **futa-tsuki,** "two months"; **to-tsuki,** "ten months."

45. The set of numerals borrowed from the Chinese is:

1. ichi (or **itsu**)	8. hachi
2. ni	9. ku (or **kyū**)
3. san	10. jū
4. shi	11. jū-ichi
5. go	12. jū-ni
6. roku (or **riku**)	13. jū-san
7. shichi	

14. jū-shi
etc.
20. ni-jū
21. ni-jū-ichi
22. ni-jū-ni
etc.
30. san-jū
40. shi-jū
etc.

100. hyaku, or ip-pyaku (lit., "one hundred")
200. ni-hyaku
etc.
1,000. sen, or is-sen (lit., "one thousand")
10,000. man, or ban, or ichi-man (lit., "one myriad")

46. These numerals cannot be used independently, but must always precede a noun, forming a sort of compound with the latter; thus: **ichi-nin,** "one person"; **it-ten** (for **ichi-ten**), "one point." As seen by these examples, the nouns with which the Chinese numerals combine are almost always of Chinese origin. Similarly, Japanese and Chinese numerals cannot be used together. **Shi,** "four," is, however, often replaced by **yo,** the native Japanese word, as in **jū-yo-nin,** "fourteen persons"; **ni-jū-yokka,** "the twenty-fourth day of the month."

AUXILIARY NUMERALS

47. "Auxiliary numeral" is the name given to a certain class of nouns with which the Chinese numerals constantly combine. They have English analogues in such expressions as "a hundred *head* of cattle," "so many *panes* of glass"; but are much more extensively used. Thus "one war-vessel" is **gunkan is-sō;** "one soldier" is **heishi ichi-mei** (or **ichi-nin**); "one pen" is **fude ip-pon** (less frequently **issō no gunkan, ichi-nin no heishi,** etc.).

48. The following are the most important auxiliary numerals:

chō, for various things with handles, such as tools, muskets, and **jinrikishas**

fū, for letters

fuku, for scrolls, sips of tea, and whiffs of tobacco

hai, for cupfuls and glassfuls

hiki, for most living creatures except human beings and birds; also for certain quantities of cloth and sums of money

hon, for cylindrical things such as sticks, trees, and fans

ka or **ko,** for things generally that have no auxiliary numeral specially appropriated to them

ken, for buildings

mai, for flat things generally

mei, for human beings

nin, for human beings

satsu, for volumes

sō, for ships

tsū, for documents

wa, for birds

NOTE.—For the euphonic changes which these auxiliary numerals undergo in composition with the numerals proper, see § 11.

49. By the Japanese themselves the names of weights and measures, such as **kin,** "a pound," are included in the same category. Thus: **ik-kin,** "one pound"; **hyak-kin,** "a hundred pounds."

50. Formerly, there existed many native Japanese auxiliary numerals which were used in combination with the native numerals proper. The only words of this class that have remained in common use are: **soroe,** for sets of things; **suji,** for ropelike things; **tomai,** for "go-downs" (e.g., **dozō mu-tomai,** "six mud go-downs"); and the isolated expressions **hitori,** "one person"; **futari,** "two persons"; and **yottari,** "four persons," which often replace **ichi-nin, ni-nin,** and **yo-nin.** Thus: **suifu futari,** "two seamen."

51. The native auxiliary numerals suffer no euphonic changes.

ORDINAL NUMBERS

52. Japanese has no separate forms for what we term the ordinals. Sometimes the cardinal numbers do duty for them;

thus: **Meiji jū-ku-nen,** "the nineteenth year of Meiji, i.e., A.D. 1886." At other times the word **dai,** "series," is prefixed, or **bamme** suffixed, to the cardinal numbers, as **dai-ichi** or **ichi bamme,** "the first." Observe such locutions as:

> **san-do,** "thrice"
> **san-do me,** "the third time"
> **san-chō me,** "third street"
> **san-nin mae,** "portions for three"
> **sam-bu no ichi,** "one-third"
> **sam-bu,** "3 per cent"
> **san wari,** "30 per cent"

> **mitsu**
> **sam-mai**
> **sam-bon** } **zutsu,** "three at a time"
> etc.

and similarly with the other numerals.

CHAPTER V

THE PARTICLE

53. The Japanese particles or expletives, in general, correspond to English particles. In some cases, however, they have a meaning similar to our adverbs or conjunctions. Other words for which English has no equivalents are included in this category. When suffixed to a verb or adjective such verb or adjective is required to be in one of the attributive forms. Exceptions to this rule will be noted.

The chief particles with their most usual significations are:

54. Ga. (*a*) **Ga** is used, as in the colloquial, as a sign of what we should call the nominative case.

b) Also, as in the colloquial, when suffixed to the attributive form of a verb at the end of a clause, it is best rendered by "yet," "but," or "still," prefixed to the following clause: **Jōin wa sōno hoan wa tsūka shitaru ga daitōryo wa shomei wo narazariki,** "The Senate passed that bill but the President did not sign it." (See **wo** [§ 61*b*], which is preferred by some writers to **ga** in such contexts.)

c) The following combinations are often seen: **ga tame ni,** "for the sake (purpose of)," **ga gotoku,** "like," "as."

55. Ka. (*a*) An interrogative particle, corresponding to our question mark, as **aru ka,** "is there?"

b) As part of the indefinite pronoun as **nanika,** "something," **tare ka,** "somebody."

c) Expression of uncertainty as **sono sodan no sadamarishi to ka nite, kondo** . . . . , "An agreement having, as it would seem, been arrived at (they are) now. . . . ."

d) When repeated usually corresponds to "either . . . . or," **Yuku ka kaeru ka, sadamezaru bekarazu,** "We must decide to either go on or to return."

e) Followed by **wa** at the end of a sentence, expressing a rhetorical question. **Sora nomi ka wa,** "Is it only that?" that is, "Of course it is not only that."

f) Suffixed to a gerund, combines with the gerundial termination **te** to signify "doubtless because," "probably on account of." Thus: **Seifu mo kanzuru tokoro arite ka, kisoku wo kaisei seri,** "The government, too, probably on account of having become aware (of this) has changed the regulations."

56. Koso. A highly emphatic particle, corresponding to an unusually strong emphasis in English, or to an inversion which puts at the beginning of the English sentence the word to which the writer desires to draw attention. This form of **koso** requires a special form of the verb ending in **e**. It is seldom seen in modern writings. Thus: **Kyoiku wa seiji no tasuke koso sure** (for indefinite **shi**) **samatage wa seji** (negative future of **suru**), "A help and not a hindrance is what education will be to the administration."

57. Mo. (*a*) Properly "also," "even."

b) Very frequently a mere expletive not needing to be translated: **en-ryo mo naku,** "without (even) any feeling of difference."

c) It is often used expletively between the two members of a compound verb: **yuki mo tsukanu uchi ni,** "before he had reached" (**yuki-tsuku,** means "to arrive at a place one is going to").

d) Likewise serves to form the hypothetical concessive mood of verbs; **yuku mo,** "even if (I) go."

e) Repeated signifies "both . . . . and," but sometimes "whether . . . . or"; **mukashi mo ima mo,** "both in ancient and modern times." **Nanji wa yuku mo yukarazu mo ware wa yukan,** "whether you go or not, I will go myself." **Mo mata** is often met with; **Kore mo mata sono ichirei nari,** "This is another of those examples."

58. To usually has the force of "that." The following uses
are noted:

1. "That" (the conjunction). Thus: **Nashi to omou,** "I
think that there are none." **To,** like the English word "that"
can never be omitted in such contexts.

2. Quotation marks; **Dai-ichi rentai to shiruseru hata,** "a
flag with the inscription 'First Regiment.'"

3. "To" followed by the infinitive: thus **kohosha to sadamuru,**
"to appoint a candidate."

4. In the semi-Chinese style, **to** is often found at the end of the
sentence in the sense of "it is said that," "he thought," etc., some
such verb as **iu, omou,** or **kiku** being understood after it. **Rondon
yori no dempō nari to,** "It is said to be a telegram from London."

5. Sometimes one of the verbal forms in **aku** as **iwaku,** "said,"
omoeraku, "thought," is placed at the commencement of the sentence which ends with **to**; thus: **Omoeraku teki kōgeki shi kitaru
beshi to,** "(He) thought that the enemy would come to the attack."

6. For the sake of emphasis, **to** is occasionally followed by the
emphatic particle **zo.**

7. **To** is usually preceded not by an attributive, but by a
conclusive verb or adjective, as seen in the foregoing example
(**nari** not **naru**). The reason is that, as it simply corresponds
to quotation marks placed after a clause or sentence complete
in itself, it does not in any way govern the preceding word.
If that word is, as it generally must be, a verb or adjective in the
conclusive form, that form remains unaffected by the presence of
to. But the fact that the postpositions generally are preceded
by an attributive verb or adjective has influenced the grammar of
to in such wise that many writers substitute the attributive for
the conclusive form when **to** follows. This happens especially
in the case of the first past, whose attributive termination **shi**
constantly replaces ·the conclusive **ki** before **to.** Thus: **Kobe
ni tochaku seshi** (for **shiki**) **to iu,** "It is said that they have
arrived at Kobe."

8. Though retaining somewhat of its force of "that," **to** must often be otherwise rendered (e.g., by "to," "into," "with," "from"), or altogether dropped in English; thus: **Aware naru arisama to nareri,** "He fell into a pitiful plight." **Musume to ninin,** "two counting my daughter" (lit., "two with my daughter"). **Kore to chigau,** "It differs from this."

9. "And"; in this sense it is generally repeated after each of the words enumerated just as in the colloquial.

59. Tote, a compound of **to,** "that," and **te,** the termination of the gerund, so that it literally signifies ". . . . ing that." It is used as an equivalent of **to iite,** "saying that"; **to omoite,** "thinking that"; **to toite,** "asking whether"; and of similar gerundial phrases. Thus: **Uchi ni kaeran tote, tachitari,** "He stood up, saying that he was going home."

Very frequently **tote** follows a verb in the conditional mood. It and the conditional termination **eba** then together signify "because . . . . said (thought, believed, etc.) to be," "on the strength of (something said, done, or imagined)"; thus: **Hito to shite mizukara i-shoku-ju wo kyu suru wa kataki koto ni arazu. Kono koto wo naseba tote, aete hokoro-beki ni arazu,** "It is not a difficult thing for a human being to provide himself with clothing, food, and shelter. He must not dare to be proud on the strength of his doing so."

60. Wa, an emphatic or separative particle. "With regard to," "so far as . . . . is concerned," are its most explicit English equivalents. But its force is generally sufficiently indicated in an English translation by an emphasis on the word to which it is suffixed, and by the placing of that word at or near the beginning of the sentence. **Te ni tazusōuru wa,** "(With regard to) the thing he holds in his hand." **Kotae-keru wa,** "He answered" (lit., "the thing he answered [was]"). In both of the foregoing examples **mono** is understood before **wa.** **Nishi wa Fuji, kita wa Tsukuba nari,** "To the west stands Mount Fuji, to the north, Mount Tsukuba." **Kono jiken wa betsu ni go hōdō itasazu,** "Concerning this matter I send no special information." **Saran**

to suru toki wa, "when about to depart." **Sono jin-in wa nen-nen kore wo sadamu,** "The number (of men) is fixed each year" (lit., "as for that number, yearly [they] fix it"). As shown in the last example, it is often convenient to render the noun followed by **wa** as a nominative in English; but it is never a nominative properly so called in the Japanese construction. It is simply a word isolated and generally placed at the head of the clause for the sake of emphasis. True nominatives or subjects are rare in Japanese, most sentences being subjectless (§§ 241, 243).

61. **Wo.** (*a*) A sign of what is in European languages named the accusative or objective case. **Kami wo shinzuru,** "to believe (in) God." **Kaze no nagu wo matsu,** "to await the getting calm of the wind," i.e., "to wait till the wind goes down."

b) When suffixed to the attributive form of a verb or adjective at the end of a clause, **wo** has an adversative force, which is generally best rendered by "yet" or "but": **Seiyo-sukuri no tsumori narishi wo, kondo aratamete Nihon-zukuri to sadameraru,** "It had been intended to build (the palace) in European style, but it has now been decided to erect a Japanese building instead." Some writers, following the usage of the colloquial, use either **ga** or **no ni** for **wo** in this case.

c) The connection between the two chief uses of **wo** is found in the fact that this particle was originally nothing more than an interjection serving, as it were, to interrupt the sentence, and draw particular attention to the word to which it was suffixed. For the same reason it is not attached to every noun which, according to European ideas of grammar, is in the accusative case; thus: **fumi kaku toki,** "when writing a letter."

d) Before the verb **suru,** "to do," it is generally absent, thus: **honyaku suru,** "to make a translation," "to translate."

e) Under (*a*) above may be classed some apparently anomalous uses of **wo** by which the student is often greatly perplexed.

1. Such phrases as **Tenno Heika wo hajime-tatematsuri,** "from His Imperial Majesty downward." Here the literal render-

ing would be: "respectfully placing His Majesty the Emperor at the beginning," a construction which we should call accusative.

2. Such phrases as **Heiwa wo ri nari to omoeba . . . . ,** "thinking that peace would be advantageous. . . . ." Here the literal rendering of the Japanese construction is "thinking (of) peace, 'it will be advantageous.'" **Heiwa** is therefore really an accusative, though rendered in English by a nominative.

3. The use of **wo** after what corresponds to the subject of an English passive verb. Thus: **Minami ni miyuru shima wo Ōshima to iu,** "The island visible to the south is called Oshima." See also the remarks on the nature of the Japanese passive verb (§ 193).

4. **Wo** at the end of a sentence. In such cases there is an inversion of the usual construction, the verb being placed at the beginning of the clause instead of at the end, for the sake of emphasis and in imitation of Chinese idiom. Thus: **Kou yoyaku no shokun wa dai-shikyu ga kamei aran koto wo** (for **Yoyaku no . . . . koto wo kou**), "We trust that gentlemen will hasten to add their names to the list of subscribers."

5. Such elliptical phrases as **Kampisei wo meizeraretari,** lit., "(They) have been commanded official expense students," i.e., "They have been commanded to become students at government expense," or more freely, "They have been notified that the expenses of their education will be defrayed by the government."

62. Ya, a particle of interrogation, doubt, or exclamation.

a) As a direct interrogative particle, its use is chiefly confined to (1) sentences which contain some other interrogative word, and (2) those in which the question asked is a purely rhetorical one, i.e., not a question properly so called, asked in order to elicit information. Thus: **Kono toki ni atatte, waga Nihon no jimmin wa ikaga subeki ya?** "In such a case how would our Japanese compatriots act?" **Karada wa koromo yori mo masareru mono narazu ya?** "Is not the body more than raiment?"

b) Its more frequent use is as a particle expressing doubt. Thus: **moshi ya,** "if perchance"; **. . . . to iu ga, sono jitsu ika**

ga ni ya, "It is said that . . . . ," "but we know not whether it be true." **Heiba no aida ni ai-miru ni itaru ya mo hakaru bekarazu,** "Who knows, perhaps we may encounter each other on the field of battle."

c) At the end of a sentence **ya** is sometimes, though rarely, a mere exclamation. **Makoto naru kana kono koto ya,** "Oh! how true these words are!"

d) Good writers sometimes (in imitation of Chinese idiom) use **ya** in a half-emphatic explanatory manner. Thus: **Teki no kogeki shi kitari ya gen wo matazu,** "We do not await the word that the enemy will come to the attack," that is, "It is not necessary to say that the enemy will attack."

e) But sometimes it sinks into a mere expletive, as **ima ya,** "now"; **kanarazu ya,** "positively."

63. The syntax of **ya** presents some anomalies, **ya** being occasionally preceded by the conclusive instead of by the attributive form of the verb or adjective, especially in the case of the present tense of adjectives, of the present tense of the verb **aru,** "to be" (conclusive **ari**), and of the present tense of the negative voice of verbs and adjectives in general. This happens chiefly when the question asked is a rhetorical one, as in the example from the New Testament above.[1] The final verb or adjective of a sentence containing **ya** is also often put in the conclusive, contrary to the general rule whereby interrogative words govern the final verb or adjective in the attributive form. The conception is more apparent than real, as it occurs almost exclusively in cases where **ya** is not properly interrogative, but has one of the meanings given above under the heading (*b*), where an example will be found (concl. **bekarazu** for attrib. **bekarazaru**). In (*d*) the conclusive is always used.

64. Zo, an emphatic particle less intense than **koso,** but best rendered in English by either of the means mentioned under **koso,** § 56.

---

[1] Cf. § 62*a* concl. **narazu** for attrib. **narazaru.**

CHAPTER VI

THE POSTPOSITION

65. Japanese postpositions correspond for the most part to English prepositions. But some words which we should call adverbs and conjunctions, and others for which English has no equivalents, are included in this category. When suffixed to a verb or adjective, postpositions require such verb or adjective to be in one of the attributive forms, a general rule which is subject to exceptions mentioned in the course of the present chapter. Postpositions are of two kinds, simple and compound.

THE SIMPLE POSTPOSITION

The chief simple postpositions, with their most usual significations, are:

66. Kara, "from," "since." **Kore kara,** "henceforward."

67. Made, "till," "as far as," "by," "down to," "to," "to such a degree." **Kore made,** "thus far," "hitherto." Such phrases as **myogonichi made** may signify either "till the day after tomorrow" or "by the day after tomorrow," but the latter meaning is the more usual.

68. Nagara. (*a*) Suffixed to nouns, signifies "just as it is," "without change," thus: **mendo nagara,** "tedious as it is," "though a bore."

b) More often it follows verbs (always in the indefinite, not in the attributive form), and then with the sense of "while," "during"; thus: **yuki-nagara,** "while going."

69. Ni, "in," "into," "to." It has a great number of idiomatic uses, of which the following are the most noteworthy:

a) What in English is called the subject of a sentence is often marked by **ni** followed by **wa** or **oite.** This gives the expression an honorific tinge, which is generally emphasized by putting the verb in the potential form, it being considered more polite to say that such and such a thing is able to happen in a person than bluntly to assert that the person did it. Thus: **Kaigun daijin ni wa saru mikka kikyo seraretari,** "The Minister of Marine returned to Tokyo on the third instant."

b) With a passive verb, **ni** corresponds to "by," donating as it does the person by whom the action is performed: **Taki ni semararuru,** "to be attacked by the enemy."

c) With a causative verb, **ni** denotes the person who is caused to perform the action; thus: **Iin ni koto wo giseshimuru,** "to cause the committee to deliberate upon a matter," i.e., "to leave a matter to the committee to deliberate upon."

d) Following the attributive form of a verb at the end of a clause, **ni** serves to indicate a contrast or difference between two consecutive actions or states, "whereupon" or "on," prefixed to the following clause, is the most literal English rendering, thus: **Futa wo toritaru ni hatashite naka no mono arazariki,** "I removed the lid whereupon as was expected the contents were missing (were not)." But more frequently **ni** in such contexts must be rendered by "but," there being hardly any difference between it and **wo** similarly placed; thus: **Kogeki shitaru ni sude ni teki wa nigetari,** "(We) attacked but the enemy had already fled."

e) **Ni** suffixed to nouns sometimes means "and." **Ju ni ken** "rifle and bayonet," **hana ni tsuki,** "flowers and moon."

f) **Ni** sometimes follows a word which according to English ideas should be in the accusative case, as: **hito ni au,** "to meet a person."

g) Suffixed to the indefinite form of the verb, **ni** signifies "in order to," "to," **tori ni yuku,** "to go to fetch."

h) Substituted for the verb **naru** after certain abstract nouns the expression corresponds to English adverbs; as **riko ni,** "cleverly."

70. Nite[1] (sometimes corrupted into **de**). (*a*) "By means of," "by," "with"; **Kore nite shiru-beshi,** "It may be hereby known."

[1] The postposition **nite** must not be confounded with **nite,** the indefinite form of the verb **naru,** which signifies "being" (§ 181).

b) "In," "at"; Ōsaka nite, "at Osaka."

71. No. (*a*) "Of," or the possessive case; thus: **Tokyo no kinko,** "the population of Tokyo"; **boku no kangae,** "my humble opinion"; **kuni wo osamuru no konnan,** "the difficulty of governing the country."

b) In examples like the following the word followed by **no** almost comes to correspond to our nominative or accusative rather than to our possessive case, and must often be turned into the subject of a clause in English. Thus: **Waga hai no tsune ni ikan to suru tokoro nari,** "It is a thing which we constantly regret." **Totsuzen dempo no kitaru ari,** "A telegram suddenly came" (lit., "Suddenly there was the coming of a telegram"). **Hito no onore wo hyo suru wo kiku,** "To hear others talk about myself."

c) While always retaining a trace of its proper meaning of "of," **no** is used in two other noteworthy idiomatic manners: (1) Between two nouns in apposition: **issaku jū-ni nichi no nichiyobi,** "The day before yesterday Sunday the twelfth." (2) Either in place of, or suffixed to, the other postpositions, it being a general rule that none of them except **no** and **ga** can show the relation between two nouns without the intervention of a verb. Thus a Japanese says: **Kono ura ni ike ari,** "There is a pond at the back of this." But he must, if the verb be omitted, say: **kono ura no ike,** "the pond *at* (lit., of) the back of this." Similarly, **kanri no kyūsokujo,** "a resting place *for* the officials; **Ei Ro no kankei,** "the relations *between* England and Russia."

d) In the following instance **no** is suffixed to the other particles or postpositions: **Pekin yori no dempō,** "a telegram from Peking"; **taiyō to chikyū to no kankei,** "the relations between the sun and the earth." Similarly when **to** in the sense of "that" or of quotation marks is followed, not by a verb, but by a noun, **no** must be inserted after it. Thus: **Kitaru to no dempō aritari,** "There was a telegram that (he) would come."

e) Not infrequently the words **tokoro no** (more rarely **no** alone) are inserted between the attributive and the noun, as in § 41.

f) Sometimes, however, **no** legitimately represents the English relative, thus: **on hanashi no kenken,** "the various matters which were mentioned by you" (lit., "the matter-matter of the honorable speaking").

72. **Ye,** "to," less often "toward," sometimes "at"; **Tokyo ye kuru,** "to come to Tokyo"; **Yokohama ye tochaku suru,** "to arrive at Yokohama."

73. **Yori,** "from," "since," "than"; **Beikoku yori,** "from America." **Hachi-ji yori kaijo,** "from eight o'clock open-place." **Sakujitsu yori,** "since yesterday." **Tsuki hana yori utsukushiki wa naki nari,** "There is nothing more beautiful than the moon and the flowers." (See also comparison of adjectives, § 103.) **Yori** always means "since" when it is suffixed to a gerund; thus: **Kono tatakai arite yori Nihon wa sekai no kyokoku to nareri,** "Since this war Japan has become a world-power."

Preceded by a negative **yori** sometimes means "unless," "except by," "without." **Ijō no jimbutsu ni arazaru yori wa kakaru jigyo wo kansei suru koto katakaru beshi,** "Except by a man of great ability it would be impossible to accomplish such an undertaking." When thus used **yori** is almost always strengthened by the addition of **wa.**

THE COMPOUND POSTPOSITION

74. Many of the postpositions can be combined in order to particularize or emphasize the sense, as **made ni,** "until," "by," or "before," for **made,** "till"; **yori mo,** "even than"; **ka aruiwa** repeated "either . . . . or." In such combinations as **no wa, no ni,** and **to wa,** an ellipsis must be supplied; thus: **Ten to (iu mono) wa,** "what is called heaven," "what is meant by the term heaven."

75. There is a large class of compound postpositions formed from nouns by prefixing **no** (less often **ga**), and generally suffixing **ni.** Thus:

76. No kage ni, "behind" (lit., "in the shadow of"). **Iwa no kage (ni),** "behind the rocks."

77. No kawari ni, "instead of," "in return for," "as compensation for," "on the other hand."

78. No tame ni, "for the sake of," "by." **Uma no tame ni keraruru,** "to be kicked by a horse."

79. No ue ni, "above" (lit., "on the top of"), "on," "besides," "after," "in relation to." **Zanji no ue (ni),** "after a short rest."

80. Ga ue ni, "over and above," "besides." **Iya ga ue ni,** "on the top of one another," "even more and more."

81. After verbs the chief word of these compound postpositions is sometimes used alone, without either **no** or **ni,** as: **Eien ni tsutōru tame,** "in order to hand it down forever."

82. There is a class of compound postpositions formed by **ni** or **wo** and a verb, the verb generally appearing as a gerund or else in the indefinite form. The most important postpositions of this class are:

83. Ni oite, "in," "on," "at." This compound postposition often serves to denote what we should call the subject of the sentence (§ 69*a*).

a) **Ni oite wa** sometimes signifies "in the event of," or "if," thus: **Shina seifu ni oite kore wo shōdaku sezaru ni oite wa,** "in the event of the Chinese government not consenting," "if the Chinese government should not consent." (In this sentence the first **ni oite** serves to mark the word which corresponds to the English nominative, while the second means "if.")

b) **Ni oite wo ya** at the end of a sentence has a very strong exclamatory force. It is generally preceded by **iwan ya** at the beginning of the sentence or clause, and should be rendered, according to circumstances, by "how much more" or "how much less"; thus: **Kiji ni oite sura sono bi kaku no gotoshi iwan ya jikkei ni** oite wa, "If it is so beautiful even in description, how much more so must it be in actual view."

84. **Ni okeru,** "in," "position in," "relations with," "compared with"; **Ei no Indo ni okeru ga gotoku,** "like England's position in India."

85. **Ni shite.** (*a*) "Being," "as," "in the capacity of"; **Gaikokujin ni shite,** "as a foreigner."

b) It is also used in many contexts where it must be translated as an adverb or an adverbial phrase: **Saiwai ni shite,** "fortunately"; **zanji ni shite,** "after a little while."

c) It is most common in the sense of "is and"; **Tokyo wa nihon no shufu ni shite Tokyo wan ni nozomu,** "Tokyo is the capital of Japan and borders on Tokyo Bay."

d) It is also sometimes used like **wo shite** in a causative construction, see § 91.

86. **Ni shite** must not be confounded with **to shite** (§ 89). **Ni shite** has the idea of long existence in a certain capacity, while **to shite** is used for "in the special capacity of." **Ni shite** is general and explanatory, **to shite** is temporary and limiting.

87. **Ni tsuki,** "with reference to," "owing to": . . . . **no gi ni tsuki,** "with reference to a matter of. . . . ."

88. **Ni yori, ni yotte,** "owing to," "because of," "by means of," "according to." **Rei ni yori,** "according to precedent," "as usual." **Kore ni yotte,** "on account of this."

89. **To shite,** "as." **Sharei to shite,** "as a token of gratitude." (See **ni shite,** § 86.)

90. **Wo motte** (lit., "having held"), "through," "by," "with," "by means of," "owing to," "because"; **Tegami wo motte,** "by letter." **Konkai taisen okorishi wo motte,** "owing to the occurrence of the recent world-war."

a) Sometimes **wo motte** sinks into being a mere sign of what we should term the accusative case, as: **Saionji ko wo motte Tokuha Zenken Daishi to nashi** . . . . , "appointing Marquis Saionji as Special Envoy Plenipotentiary."

b) **Motte** without **wo** generally signifies "and thereby," "and thus."

c) But both **wo motte** and **motte** may often be neglected in translating, though some trace of their proper meaning generally lingers in the original Japanese; thus: **Guntai wo moke motte kokka wo hogo su,** "We raise troops to (and thereby) protect our native land." **Hanahada motte,** "very"; **Ima motte,** "now," "down to the present."

d) **Wo motte suru** properly means "to use," but it can often be dropped in translation: **Waga hai no miru tokoro wo motte suru ni,** "looking at it from our point of view" (lit., "using the seeing place of our company").

e) **Wo motte nari** means "it is because of."

f) **Kore wo motte,** "on this account," "for this reason," "therefore."

g) **Omomuki wo motte,** "with regard to," "in respect to."

91. Wo shite. (*a*) With a causative verb serves to denote the person who is caused to perform the action (§ 206). Thus **Dai shichi shidan wo shite kōgeki seshimeki,** "He caused the seventh division to attack."

b) Occasionally the noun corresponding to the English nominative is marked by the addition of **wo shite,** as: **Moshi Kairiku un-yu no jotai wo shite, kaku no gotoku fukanzen naru koto nakarashimeba,** "if the state of communications by sea and land were not so imperfect as they are."

92. Ya mo, "whether . . . . may (might) not," . . . . **ni itaru ya mo shiru bekarazu,** "We cannot tell whether it may not result in. . . . ."

93. Ya wo: in this combination **ya** has its original interrogative sense, and **wo** serves to show that the whole clause preceding it is the object of the following verb: **Nani ga yue ni furuwazarishi ya wo tankyu suru ni,** lit., "on investigating (this thing) because of what did it not exercise influence?" i.e., "on inquiring into the reasons for its lack of success."

94. The general rule, according to which particles and post-positions must be preceded by the attributive form of the verb or adjective, admits of a few exceptions in special locutions, besides those noted before under **ka, ni, to,** etc.; thus: **ari no mama** (for **aru mama**), "just as it is," **nashi ni** (for **naki ni**), "without"; and such idioms as **furi mo sede** or **furi wa sede,** "not raining"; **Kuwashiku wa zonzezu,** " (I) know not exactly," where the indefinite form precedes **mo** and **wa.**

CHAPTER VII
THE ADJECTIVE
PRIMARY ADJECTIVE FORMS

95. The inflections of Japanese adjectives do not, like the inflections of English adjectives, serve to distinguish the degree of comparison. Neither do they, as in French, indicate number or gender. Number and gender are considerations to which the Japanese grammatical system pays little or no heed. The object of the inflections of Japanese adjectives (and verbs) is primarily to show whether the force of the adjective (or verb) is attributive or predicative, indefinite or conclusive; and secondly, to mark distinctions of tense and mood. All adjectives contain the verb "to be" implicitly. Thus: **Umi fukashi,** "The sea (is) deep."

In its simple state, a Japanese adjective has four forms, viz.:

96. The stem which is used only in compounds as **hoso-nagaki,** "narrow-long," i.e., "slender"; **yo-suguru,** "to be too good."

97. The indefinite or adverbial form, which is obtained by adding **ku** to the stem. It is used in two distinct manners, viz.:

a) To qualify a verb as: **Hayaku kuru,** "to come quickly." In this case it corresponds to the English adverb in *ly*. But the Japanese use this form even before such verbs as "to be" and "to become," where English idiom requires the corresponding adjective. Thus: **Utuskushiku naru beshi,** "It will become beautiful."

b) As itself a predicative verb in every clause of a sentence except the last. Thus: **Yama takaku, kikō samuku, jinka sukunashi,** "The mountains (of a certain country) are high, its climate is cold, and human dwellings few." In such cases each Japanese adjective in **ku** must be rendered by the corresponding

English adjective preceded by some tense of the verb "to be."
The essential characteristic of the indefinite form is that it has
no tense or mood.   In order to know by what tense or mood to
translate it into English, it is necessary to ascertain the tense or
mood of the adjective or verb nearest after it which is not also in
the same indefinite form.   Sometimes this will be the last adjective or verb of the whole sentence, sometimes only the adjective
or verb of the last of a set of similar clauses.   Thus in the foregoing example **takaku** and **samuku** must be translated by the
English present indicative, because of the final adjective **sukunashi** makes a general assertion, and may therefore be considered
to be in the present tense.   Again, take the example: **Toshi
wakaku, karada mo tsuyokereba, gunjin ni teki su-beshi,** "Being
young and strong, he will be suitable for a soldier."   Here the
intervention of the adjective **tsuyokereba** in the conditional mood
at the end of the succeeding clause shows that **wakaku** also must
be construed as a conditional (**wakakereba**).   The construction
is often a little more complicated.   Thus: **Fune aredomo hito
naku: hito aru mo kikai nakariki,** "We had ships, but no men;
and even if we had had the men, we had no machinery."   Here
the rhythm of the sentence shows that we must go to the end of
the clause **hito aru mo, kikai nakariki** to find the adjective (verb)
corresponding to **naku.**   The **aru** of the second clause has to be
passed over.

98. The conclusive form, which is obtained by adding **shi** to
the stem.   It is used only as a predicative, as in the case of
sukunashi in the first example given in the preceding paragraph.
Those adjectives whose stem ends in **shi** or **ji** do not add another
shi to form the conclusive, the one **shi** being held to suffice.
Thus: **mezurashiku,** conclusive **mezurashi,** "strange"; **aru-
majiku,** conclusive **aru-maji,** "should not be."   This exception is
sometimes disregarded by ignorant writers; and such ungram-
matical forms as **ashishi** (for **ashi**), "bad," are therefore occasionally met with.

99. The attributive form, which is obtained by adding **ki** to the stem. It is used in three distinct manners.

a) To qualify a noun, as **yoroshiki hōhō,** "a good method"; **aru-majiki koto,** "a thing that ought not to be" (lit., "an ought-not-to-be thing").

b) When the adjective is followed by a postposition, thus: **hōhō no yoroshiki yori** (colloq., **shikata ga yoroshii kara**), "owing to the excellence of the method"; **Mijikaki mo yoshi,** "Though (it is) short, it is good." **Yoshi** is the conclusive form of the adjective **yoki.** It will be noticed that the attributive form of the adjective, when thus used, ceases to be an adjective according to European ideas, and corresponds rather to an English abstract substantive, or to an adjective preceded by the verb "to be." The abstract substantive in **sa,** so common in the colloquial, is almost always replaced in the written language by the attributive form, as **samuki** for **samusa,** "the cold."

c) At the end of a clause or sentence, when one of the preceding words of the clause or sentence is an interrogative. Thus: **Susumu to shirizoku to izure ka yoki?** "To advance or to retreat, which is better?"

100. The paradigm of the primary forms of adjectives is as follows:

	STEM	INDEFINITE FORM	CONCLUSIVE FORM	ATTRIBUTIVE FORM	
The majority of adjectives	haya	hayaku	hayashi	hayaki	"early"
	go to	gotoku	gotoshi	gotoki	"like"
	be	beku	beshi	beki	{ "able" / "must" }
	na	naku	nashi	naki	{ "non-existent" / "is not" }
Adjectives whose stem ends in **shi** or **ji**	yoroshi	yoroshiku	yoroshi	yoroshiki	"good"
	maji	majiku	maji	majiki	{ "unable" / "must not" }

TENSE AND MOOD IN THE ADJECTIVE

101. Being of the nature of a verb, the Japanese adjective is inflected to indicate tense and mood. The conclusive and attributive forms explained above may be termed its present tense, while the indefinite form is of no tense in particular, serving as it does to suspend the meaning until the end of the sentence be reached.

102. The memory will be assisted by noting that most of the tenses of the affirmative voice and all the tenses of the negative are formed by agglutinating the various inflections of the verb **aru**, "to be," to the indefinite form (**hayaku**), the vowel **u** of the latter being dropped, and the vowel **a** of the former being in some tenses changed into **e**; furthermore, that **beku, beki, beshi,** the suffix forming the potential mood (§ 119), is itself an adjective regularly conjugated through most of the tenses.

COMPARISON OF ADJECTIVES

103. Comparison in Japanese is more often implicit than explicit. Thus, when referring to the relative height of Fujiyama and Asamayama, a Japanese will not say, "Fujiyama is the higher," but simply, "Mount Fuji is high" (**Fuji wa takashi**), that is, in comparison with the other mountain mentioned. Indeed, even in English the so-called positive is often a comparative by implication; for when we say, for instance, that "Such and such a person is old," we mean that he is older than most other people. Comparison may, however, be made explicit in Japanese by using the postposition **yori**, "than" (properly "from"). Thus: **Fuji wa Asama yori takashi,** lit., "As for Fuji, than Asama, it is high," i.e., "Fuji is high as considered from the standpoint of Asama." Again: **Asama wa Fuji yori takakarazu,** "As for Asama, it is not high as considered from the standpoint of Fuji," i.e., "Asama is less high than Fuji." If three or more mountains were spoken of, we should have what in English is termed the superlative; the Japanese idiom remains the same. Here is another example: **Tenka no yama kore yori takaki wa nashi,** "There is no higher mountain than this" (lit., "world's mountains, this than, high is-not").

104. When not simply implied, or expressed by **yori,** the comparative and superlative may be indicated by prefixing to the positive some such word as **nao,** "still more"; **itatte,** "extremely"; **oi ni,** "greatly"; **sukoburu,** "very"; **kiwamete,** "extremely." The superlative form is also sometimes indicated by suffixing the word **sem-ban,** "a thousand myriads," thus: **kinodoku semban,** "inexpressibly sorry."

105. Excess of a quality is, like the comparative and superlative, generally denoted by the adjective in its simple form; thus: "This is too high" will be in Japanese simply "This is high" (**Kore wa takashi**), viz.: by implication, higher than it ought to be. The expression may be rendered more explicit by suffixing the verb **suguru** to the adjective stem, as **taka-suguru,** lit., "to go past in height." The word **amari,** "excessive" may also be used, prefixed to the simple adjective; thus: **Amari takashi,** "altogether too high," but this is rare.

PARADIGM OF ADJECTIVES
106. Hayaki, "early" (stem haya), affirmative voice.

a) Indefinite Form for All
       Tenses..............hayaku

Indicative—

b) Present: Conclusive....hayashi.................(I, you, he, she, it, we, they)
        Attributive........hayaki   am, are, or is early

c) Past: Conclusive.......hayakariki...............(I, etc.) was or were early
        Attributive........hayakarishi

d) Future: Conclusive.....hayakaran...............(I, etc.) shall or will be early
        Attributive........hayakaran

Oblique—

e) Conditional...........hayakereba..............as, since, or when (I, etc.)
                                                       am, etc., early

f) Hypothetical..........hayaku(m)ba............if (I, etc.) am, etc., early

g) Actual Concessive......hayakeredomo...........though (I, etc.) am, etc.,
                                                       early

h) Hypothetical Concessive hayaku mo..............though (I, etc.) should be
                                                       early

i) Imperative...........hayakare................be early

j) Gerund...............hayakute...............having been early (by)
                                                       being early

POTENTIAL FORMS

k) Indefinite Form for All
       Tenses..............hayaku
                            hayakaru-beku

Indicative—

l) Present: Conclusive....hayakaru-beshi..........(I, etc.) will, shall, would,
        Attributive........hayakaru-beki   should, may, might, can,
                                                        could, or ought to be
                                                        early

m) Past: Conclusive.......hayakaru-bekariki........(I, etc.) should, etc., have
        Attributive........hayakaru-bekarishi   been early

Oblique—

n) Conditional ....hayakaru-bekereba.......as, or since (I, etc.) may be
                                                       early

o) Hypothetical..........hayakaru-beku(m)ba.....if (I, etc.) may be early

p) Actual Concessive......hayakaru-bekeredomo....though (I, etc.) may be early

q) Hypothetical Concessive hayakaru-beku mo.......though (I, etc.) may per-
                                                       haps be early

r) The imperative form of the adjective is scarcely used except in a few set phrases
       such as Yokare ashikare, "be it good or bad," "for better or worse"

s) Causative Verbal Form hayakarashimuru (§ 203)..(I, etc.) cause (someone) to
                                                       be early

PARADIGM OF ADJECTIVES

107. Hayaki, "early" (stem haya), negative voice.

a) Indefinite Form for All
    Tenses.............. hayakarazu

Indicative—

b) Present: Conclusive.... hayakarazu.............. (I, you, he, she, it, we, they)
    Attributive........ hayakarazaru   am, are, or is not early

c) Past: Conclusive....... hayakarazariki........... (I, etc.) was or were not
    Attributive........ hayakarazarishi   early

d) Future: Conclusive..... hayakarazaran........... (I, etc.) shall or will not be
    Attributive........ hayakarazaran   early

Oblique—

e) Conditional........... hayakarazareba.......... as, since, or when (I, etc.)
     am, was, or is not early

f) Hypothetical.......... hayakarazu(m)ba........ if (I, etc.) am, etc., not
     early

g) Actual Concessive...... hayakarazaredomo*....... though (I, etc.) am, etc.,
     not early

h) Hypothetical Concessive hayakarazaru mo .... though (I, etc.) should not
     be early

POTENTIAL FORMS

i) Indefinite Form for All
    Tenses.............. hayakaru-bekarazu

Indicative—

j) Present: Conclusive.... hayakaru-bekarazu....... (I, etc.) will, shall, would,
    Attributive........ hayakaru-bekarazaru   should, may, might, can,
     could, ought to, not be
     early

k) Past: Conclusive....... hayakaru-bekarazariki.... (I, etc.) should, etc., not
    Attributive........ hayakaru-bekarazarishi   have been early

Oblique—

l) Conditional........... hayakaru-bekarazareba...as or since (I, etc.) should,
     etc., not be early

m) Hypothetical.......... hayakaru-bekarazu(m)ba..if, (I, etc.) should, etc., not
     be early

n) Concessive........... hayakaru-
     bekarazaredomo*...... though (I, etc.) should, etc.,
     not be early

o) The Causative Negative
    Form.............. hayakarazarashimuru
     § (204) .... (I, etc.) cause (someone) not
     to be early

* In the concessive forms mo is often omitted from the termination domo.

CHAPTER VIII

THE VERB

INTRODUCTORY REMARKS

108. The functions of the Japanese verb differ in some important respects from those of the verbs of European languages. Distinctions of person and number are utterly foreign to it. On the other hand, many of the tenses have two forms—an attributive and a conclusive—while there is a general indefinite form which does duty for all the tenses. *The verb and adjective thus closely resemble each other; and it is impossible to understand the grammar of the verb, unless the considerations advanced in the chapter on adjectives have been thoroughly mastered.*

To recapitulate briefly what has there been set forth:

109. The indefinite form stands at the end of each member of a set of clauses excepting the final member; and the tense or mood by which it should be rendered can only be known when the verb or adjective of that final clause is reached; thus: **Natsu kitari, haru yuku,** "Summer comes and spring goes." Here the indefinite form **kitari** must be rendered by the present, because the final verb **yuku** is in the present. (See first conjugation, § 118.) The indefinite form of verbs is likewise used to form compounds (in adjectives it is the stem that performs this function), as **kitari-tou,** "to come and ask," and **tsuge-tamau,** "to deign to inform" (**tsuge** being indefinite form of **tsuguru,** second conjugation, § 134).

110. The conclusive forms stand only at the end of a sentence. Thus: **Hito kitareri,** "The people have come" (first conjugation, § 118c).

111. The attributive forms serve to qualify nouns, herein resembling the participles of European languages. Thus: **Kitareru hito,** lit., "the have-come people," i.e., "the people who

[44]

have come." They are, moreover, used substantively, like adjectives followed by postpositions, thus: **Hito no kitareru wo mite,** lit., "seeing the having come of people," i.e., "seeing that people had come."

112. What obscures this threefold distinction and thereby perplexes the beginner is the fact that some of the tenses which are capable of being used both as conclusives and as attributives have but one inflection to perform the two functions, as see **yuku,** § 118*b*. Furthermore, the modern colloquial of Tokyo has dropped all distinctively conclusive forms, thereby introducing a second element of confusion for those who acquire the colloquial before commencing the study of the written language. The student acquainted with the colloquial should specially note that the written language has no such forms in the present tense of verbs of the second and third conjugations as **homeru, ireru,** or **sugiru.** These are replaced, according to circumstances, by

homu		homuru	
iru	Conclusive	iruru	Attributive
sugu		suguru	

113. When there are two verbs derived from the same stem, such as **iru,** "to go in," and **iruru** (colloquial **ireru**), "to put in," one belonging to the first conjugation, and the other to the second, the conclusive form of the present tense is therefore identical in both. Thus **iru,** at the end of a sentence, may signify either "goes in" or "put in," according to circumstances. In the case of the attributive form there is no ambiguity, as it is **iru,** "goes in," in the first conjugation, and **iruru,** "puts in," in the second.

114. Note that the attributive form serves to take the place of the relative pronoun in Japanese. The way their absence is provided for may be seen by the foregoing example of **kitareru** and by the following: **yukishi hito,** "the person who went" (lit., "the went person"), and **shiru-beki koto,** "a thing which should be known" (lit., "a should-be-known thing").

[45]

115. As seen by these examples, the verb or adjective of the relative clause must be put in the attributive form. If there are several relative clauses, then only the verb or adjective of the last clause takes the attributive form, all the preceding clauses having the verb or adjective in the indefinite form.

CONJUGATION OF VERBS

116. All the inflections are added to the stem, which is itself invariable. Some of the inflections consist of a single vowel, whose original meaning is obscure, as in **yuki, yuku, yuke.** But by far the greater number are obtained by agglutinating fragments of old auxiliary verbs, and in some few cases particles, postpositions, and adjectives, to the single vowel forms; thus: **yukiki, yuki-tari, yuku-beshi, yukeba** (§ 102).

117. There are four regular conjugations of Japanese verbs.

a) To the first conjugation belong the great majority of true, underived verbs.

b) In the second conjugation the number of true verbs is small.

c) The verbs belonging to the third conjugation are also few in number and little used.

d) The fourth conjugation consists of the following ten dissyllabic verbs only:

> **hiru,** "to dry in the sun"
> **hiru,** "to winnow"
> **hiru,** "to sneeze"
> **iru,** "to shoot with a bow and arrow"
> **iru,** "to fuse or cast metal"
> **iru,** "to dwell"
> **kiru,** "to wear," "to put on," "to have on"
> **miru,** "to look," "to see"
> **niru,** "to resemble"
> **niru,** "to boil"

Kaerimiru, "to look back," "to consider," follows **miru** from which it is compounded. **Kokoromuru** (colloquial **kokoromiru**), "to test," though also derived from **miru,** follows the third conjugation.

FIRST REGULAR CONJUGATION

118. Verb, **yuku**, "to go" (stem **yuk**), active affirmative voice.

a) Indefinite Form for All
Tenses..............**yuki**

Indicative—

b) Present: Conclusive....**yuku**....................(I, you, he, she, it, we, they)
Attributive........**yuku**   go

c) Perfect: Conclusive....**yukeri‡**............../........(I, etc.) went, have gone, or
Attributive........**yukeru**   had gone

d) First Past: Conclusive..**yukiki**.................(I, etc.) went, have gone, or
Attributive........**yukishi**   had gone

e) Second Past: Conclusive **yukitari**.................(I, etc.) went, have gone, or
Attributive........**yukitaru**   had gone

f) Third Past: Conclusive **yukitariki**...............(I, etc.) went, have gone, or
Attributive........**yukitarishi**   had gone

g) Fourth Past: Conclusive **yukinu**.................(I, etc.) went, have gone, or
Attributive........**yukinuru**   had gone away

h) Future: Conclusive.....**yukan, yukinan**..........(I, etc.) shall or will prob-
Attributive........or **yuku naran**   ably go

Oblique—

i) Present Conditional....**yukeba**.................as, since, or when (I, etc.) go

j) Past Conditional.......**yukishikaba**.............as, since, or when (I, etc.)
                     yukitareba   went, have gone, or had
                                                               gone

k) Present Hypothetical...**yukaba**..................if (I, etc.) go
                     yukinaba
                     yuku naraba

l) Past Hypothetical......**yukitaraba**..............if (I, etc.) had gone
                     yukishi naraba

m) Optative.............**yukabaya**...............Oh, that I could go!

n) Present Actual*........**yukedomo**...............though (I, etc.) do actually
Concessive.........**yuku to iedomo**   go

o) Present Hypothetical...**yuku mo†**..............even if (I, etc.) go
Concessive.........**yukite mo**

p) Past Concessive........**yukishikadomo**...........though (I, etc.) went, have
                     yukitaredomo   gone, or had gone
                     yukitari to iedomo
                     yukishi to iedomo
                     yukishi mo

q) Imperative...........**yuke**....................go!

r) Gerund..............**yukite**.................(by) having gone, (by) going

* **Mo** may be omitted in all concessive tenses.
† Sometimes **yukan naredomo**.
‡ **Yukere** is found in poetry.

FIRST REGULAR CONJUGATION

119. Verb, **yuku,** "to go" (stem **yuk**), active affirmative voice
—*continued.*

POTENTIAL FORMS

Indicative—
a) Indefinite Form........**yuku-beku**
b) Present: Conclusive....**yuku-beshi***.............(I, etc.) will, shall, would,
     Attributive........**yuku-beki**   should, may, might, can,
                     could, must, or ought to go
c) Past: Conclusive.......**yuku-bekariki**...........(I, etc.) should, etc., have
     Attributive........**yuku-bekarishi**   gone
Oblique—
d) Conditional...........**yuku-bekereba**...........as, since (I, etc.) should,
                      etc., go
e) Hypothetical..........**yuku-beku(m)ba**.........if (I, etc.) should, etc., go
f) Actual Concessive.....**yuku-bekeredomo**........though (I, etc.) should, etc.,
           yuku-beshi to iedomo   go
g) Hypothetical Concessive **yuku-beku mo**...........even if (I, etc.) should, etc.,
                      go

DESIDERATIVE FORMS

Indicative—
h) Indefinite Form.......**yuki-taku**
i) Present: Conclusive....**yuki-tashi**..............(I, etc.) want to go
     Attributive........**yuki-taki**
j) Past: Conclusive......**yuki-takariki**.............(I, etc.) wanted to go
     Attributive........**yuki-takarishi**
Oblique—
k) Conditional...........**yuki-takereba**...........as, since, or when (I, etc.)
                      want to go
l) Hypothetical..........**yuki-taku(m)ba**..........if (I, etc.) want to go
m) Concessive..........**yuki-takeredomo**........though (I, etc.) want to go
           yuki-tashi to iedomo

ILLATIVE FORMS

Indicative—
n) Past: Conclusive.......**yuki-keri**...............(I, etc.) went, have gone, or
     Attributive........**yuki-keru**   had gone
Oblique—
o) Conditional..........**yuki-kereba**.............as, since, or when (I, etc.)
                      went, have gone, or had
                      gone
p) Concessive...........**yuki-keredomo**...........though (I, etc.) went, have
                      gone, or had gone

* Sometimes **yukimi-beshi.**

THE VERB

FIRST REGULAR CONJUGATION

120. Verb, **yuku**, "to go" (stem **yuk**), active negative voice.

Indicative—

a) Present: Conclusive....**yukazu**..................(I, you, he, she, it, we, you,
    yukazaru   they) do not go
    Attributive........**yukanu**

b) Past: Conclusive......**yukazariki** ....(I, etc.) did not go, have
    Attributive........**yukazarishi**   not gone, or had not gone

c) Future: Conclusive.....**yukazaran** or **yukaji**.......(I, etc.) shall or will not go
    Attributive........**yukazaran** or **yukaji**

Oblique—

d) Present Conditional....**yukazareba**..............as, since, or when (I, etc.)
    yukaneba   do not go

e) Past Conditional.......**yukazarishikaba**..........as, since, or when (I, etc.)
    yukazarishi ni yotte   did not go, have not
        gone, or had not gone

f) Present Hypothetical...**yukazu(m)ba**...........if (I, etc.) do not go

g) Past Hypothetical......**yukazariseba**...........if (I, etc.) had not gone
    yukazarishi naraba

h) Present Actual
    Concessive.........**yukazaredomo**..........though (I, etc.) do not go
    yukanedomo
    yukazu to iedomo

i) Present Hypothetical
    Concessive.........**yukazaru mo**.............even if (I, etc.) do not go

j) Past Concessive.......**yukazarishikadomo**.......though (I, etc.) did not go,
    yukazarishi to iedomo   have not gone, or had not
    yukazarishi naredomo   gone
    yukazarishi mo

k) Imperative...........**yukazare**..............go not, do not go!
    yuku nakare
    yuku-na
    yuku koto nakare

l) Gerund..............**yukazu**.................(by) not having gone, (by)
    yukazu ni   not going
    yukazu shite
    yukade

m) The Causative Negative
    Form..............**yukazarashimuru** (§ 204)..(I, etc.) cause (some person)
    not to go

FIRST REGULAR CONJUGATION

121. Verb, **yuku,** "to go" (stem **yuk**), active negative voice
—*continued.*

POTENTIAL FORMS

Indicative—
a) Indefinite Form........**yuku-bekarazu**
b) Present: Conclusive....**yuku-bekarazu**...........(I, etc.) will, shall, would,
    Attributive........**yuku-bekarazaru**   should, may, might, or
                                 ought not to go
c) Past: Conclusive......**yuku-bekarazariki**........(I, etc.) should not, etc.,
    Attributive........**yuku-bekarazarishi**   have gone
Oblique—
d) Conditional...........**yuku-bekarazareba**.......as, or since I (etc.) should
                               not, etc., go
e) Hypothetical..........**yuku-bekarazu(m)ba**.....if (I,etc.) should not,etc.,go
f) Actual Concessive......**yuku-bekarazaredomo**....though (I, etc.) should not,
              yuku-bekarazu* to iedomo   etc., go
g) Hypothetical Concessive **yuku-bekarazaru mo**......even if (I, etc.) should, etc.,
                              not go

PROHIBITIVE FORMS

Indicative—
h) Indefinite Form........**yuku-majiku**†
i) Present: Conclusive....**yuku-maji**
    Attributive........**yuku-majiki**
j) Past: Conclusive......**yuku-majikariki**   Same renderings as for
    Attributive........**yuku-majikarishi**   corresponding Potential
Oblique—   Forms
k) Conditional...........**yuku-majikereba**
l) Hypothetical..........**yuku-majiku(m)ba**
m) Concessive...........**yuku-majikeredomo**

ILLATIVE FORMS

Indicative—
n) Past: Conclusive......**yukazari-keri**.............(I, etc.) did not go, have
    Attributive........**yukazari-keru**   not gone, or had not gone
Oblique—
o) Conditional...........**yukazari-kereba**..........as, since, or when (I, etc.)
                                 did not go, have not
                                 gone, or had not gone
p) Concessive...........**yukazari-keredomo**.......though(I, etc.) did not go,
                                 have not gone, or had not
                                 gone

* Sometimes **yukazaru-beshi** (§ 172).
† At present the use of forms in **maji** is largely confined to epistolary writings.

FIRST REGULAR CONJUGATION

122. Verb, **kiru,** "to cut," passive affirmative voice* (stem **kir,** sign of passive **ar,** remainder of inflections same as for second conjugation).

a) Indefinite Form for All
    Tenses.............**kirare**

Indicative—
b) Present: Conclusive....**kiraru**.................(I, you, she, it, we, they)
    Attributive........**kiraruru**   am, are, or is cut
c) First Past: Conclusive..**kirareki**.................(I, etc.) was, have, has, or
    Attributive........**kirareshi**   had been cut
d) Second Past: Conclusive **kiraretari**...............(I, etc.) was, etc., cut
    Attributive........**kiraretaru**
e) Third Past: Conclusive **kiraretariki**.............(I, etc.) was, etc., cut
    Attributive........**kiraretarishi**
f) Fourth Past: Conclusive **kirarenu**................(I, etc.) was, etc., cut
    Attributive........**kirarenuru**
g) Future: Conclusive.....**kiraren, kirarenan** or......(I, etc.) shall or will prob-
    Attributive........**kiraruru naran**   ably be cut

Oblique—
h) Present Conditional....**kirarureba**...............as, since, or when (I, etc.)
                 am, etc., cut
i) Past Conditional.......**kirareshikaba**...........as, since, or when (I, etc.)
           kiraretareba   was, etc., cut
j) Present Hypothetical...**kirareba**.................if (I, etc.) am, etc., cut
           kirarenaba
           kiraruru naraba
k) Past Hypothetical......**kiraretaraba**.............if (I, etc.) had been cut
           kirareshi naraba
l) Optative.............**kirarebaya**...............Oh that I could be cut!
m) Present Actual
    Concessive.........**kiraruredomo**............though (I, etc.) will actually
           kiraru to iedomo   be cut
n) Present Hypothetical
    Concessive.........**kiraruru mo**.............even if (I, etc.) be cut
           kirarete mo
o) Past Concessive.......**kirareshikadomo**.........though (I, etc.), was, etc.,
           kiraretaredomo   cut
           kiraretari to iedomo
           kirareshi to iedomo
           kirareshi mɔ

p) Imperative...........**kirareyo**................be cut!
q) Gerund..............**kirarete**.................(by) having been cut, (by) being cut

* Used also as a potential and honorific. See §§ 189 and 194.

FIRST REGULAR CONJUGATION

123. Verb, **kiru,** "to cut," passive affirmative voice—*continued.*

POTENTIAL FORMS

Indicative—

a) Indefinite Form........ **kiraru-beku**

b) Present: Conclusive.... **kiraru-beshi**.............(I, etc.) will, shall, would,
     Attributive........ **kiraru-beki**   should, may, might, can,
                                      could, must, or ought to
                                      be cut

c) Past: Conclusive....... **kiraru-bekariki**...........(I, etc.) should, etc., have
     Attributive........ **kiraru-bekarishi**   been cut

Oblique—

d) Conditional .... **kiraru-bekereba**..........as, or since (I, etc.) should,
                                        etc., be cut

e) Hypothetical.......... **kiraru-beku(m)ba**........if (I, etc.) should, etc., be
                                        cut

f) Actual Concessive...... **kiraru-bekeredomo**.......though (I, etc.) should, etc.,
             kiraru-beshi to iedomo   be cut

g) Hypothetical Concessive **kiraru-beku mo**..........even if (I, etc.) should, etc.
                                       be cut

DESIDERATIVE FORMS

Indicative—

h) Indefinite Form........ **kirare-taku**

i) Present: Conclusive.... **kirare-tashi**.............(I, etc.) want to be cut
     Attributive........ **kirare-taki**

j) Past: Conclusive....... **kirare-takariki**..........(I, etc.) wanted to be cut
     Attributive........ **kirare-takarishi**

Oblique

k) Conditional........... **kirare-takereba**..........as, since, or when (I, etc.)
                                        want to be cut

l) Hypothetical.......... **kirare-taku(m)ba**........if (I, etc.) want to be cut

m) Concessive........... **kirare-takeredomo**.......though (I, etc.) want to be
             kirare-tashi to iedomo   cut

ILLATIVE FORMS

Indicative—

n) Past: Conclusive....... **kirare-keri**..............(I, etc.) was, etc., cut
     Attributive........ **kirare-keru**

Oblique—

o) Conditional........... **kirare-kereba**............as, since, or when (I, etc.)
                                        was, etc., cut

p) Concessive........... **kirare-keredomo**.........though (I, etc.) was, etc., cut

FIRST REGULAR CONJUGATION

124. Verb, **kiru,** "to cut," passive negative voice (stem **kir,** sign of passive **ar,** remainder of inflections as in second conjugation).

Indicative—

a) Present: Conclusive.... **kirarezu**.................(I, you, he, she, it, we, they)
  Attributive........**kirarenu**   am, are, or is not cut
     kirarezaru
b) Past: Conclusive.......**kirarezariki**..............(I, etc.) was not cut, have
  Attributive........**kirarezarishi**   not been cut, or had not been cut
c) Future: Conclusive.....**kirarezaru** or **kirareji**.....(I, etc.) shall or will not be
  Attributive........**kirarezaran** or **kirareji**   cut
Oblique—
d) Present Conditional....**kirarezareba**   as, since, or when (I, etc.)
     kirareneba   am, etc., not cut
e) Past Conditional.......**kirarezarishikaba**.........as, since, or when (I, etc.)
     kirarezarishi ni yotte   am not cut, have not been cut, or had not been cut
f) Present Hypothetical...**kirarezu(m)ba**............if (I, etc.) am, etc., not cut
g) Past Hypothetical......**kirarezariseba**............if (I, etc.) had not been cut
     kirarezarishi naraba
h) Present Actual
  Concessive..........**kirarezaredomo**..........though (I, etc.) am, etc.,
     kirarenedomo   not cut
     kirarezu to iedomo
i) Present Hypothetical
  Concessive..........**kirarezaru mo**...........even if (I, etc.) am, etc., not cut
j) Past Concessive........**kirarezarishikadomo**......though (I, etc.) am not cut,
     kirarezarishi to iedomo   have not been cut, or had not been cut
     kirarezarishi naredomo
     kirarezarishi mo
k) Imperative...........**kirarezare**..............be cut not, will not be cut
     kiraruru nakare
     kiraruru-na
     kiraruru koto nakare
l) Gerund..............**kirarezu**................(by) not having been cut,
     kirarezu ni   (by) not being cut
     kirarezu shite
     kirarede

FIRST REGULAR CONJUGATION

125. Verb, kiru, "to cut," passive negative voice—*continued.*

POTENTIAL FORMS

Indicative—
a) Indefinite Form........kiraru-bekarazu
b) Present: Conclusive....kiraru-bekarazu..........(I, etc.) will, shall, would,
        Attributive........kiraru-bekarazaru   should, may, might, can,
                                                      could, must, or ought not
                                                      to be cut
c) Past: Conclusive.......kiraru-bekarazariki.......(I, etc.) should **not**, etc.,
        Attributive........kiraru-bekarazarishi   have been cut
Oblique—
d) Conditional...........kiraru-bekarazareba......as, or since (I, etc.) should
                                                  not, etc., be cut
e) Hypothetical..........kiraru-bekarazu(m)ba.....if (I, etc.) should **not**, etc.,
                                                  be cut
f) Actual Concessive......kiraru-bekarazaredomo....though (I, etc.) should not,
                      kiraru-bekarazu to iedomo   etc., be cut
g) Hypothetical Concessive kiraru-bekarazaru mo.....even if (I, etc.) should, etc.,
                                                  not be cut

PROHIBITIVE FORMS

Indicative—
h) Indefinite Form.......kiraru-majiku
i) Present: Conclusive....kiraru-maji
        Attributive........kiraru-majiki
j) Past: Conclusive.......kiraru-majikariki
        Attributive........kiraru-majikarishi   Same renderings as for
Oblique—   corresponding Potential
k) Conditional...........kiraru-majikereba   Forms
l) Hypothetical..........kiraru-majiku(m)ba
m) Concessive...........kiraru-majikeredomo

ILLATIVE FORMS

Indicative—
n) Past: Conclusive.......kirarezari-keri...........(I, etc.) was not cut, have
        Attributive........kirarezari-keru   not been cut, or had **not**
                                                been cut
Oblique—
o) Conditional...........kirarezari-kereba.........as, since, or when (I, etc.)
                                              was not cut, have not, or
                                            had not been cut
p) Concessive...........kirarezari-keredomo......though (I, etc.) was not cut,
                                              have not been cut, or had
                                            not been cut

FIRST REGULAR CONJUGATION

126. Verb, **kiru,** "to cut," causative affirmative voice (stem **kir,** sign of causative **ashim,*** remainder of inflections as in second conjugation).

a) Indefinite Form for All
Tenses..............**kirashime**

Indicative—

b) Present: Conclusive....**kirashimu**...............(I, you, he, she, it, we, they)
Attributive........**kirashimuru**   causet to cut

c) First Past: Conclusive..**kirashimeki**..............(I, etc.) caused, have, or
Attributive........**kirashimeshi**   had causedt to cut

d) Second Past: Conclusive **kirashimetari**............(I, etc.) caused, etc.,t to cut
Attributive........**kirashimetaru**

e) Third Past: Conclusive..**kirashimetariki**..........(I, etc.) caused, etc.,t to cut
Attributive........**kirashimetarishi**

f) Fourth Past: Conclusive **kirashimenu**.............(I, etc.) caused, etc.,t to cut
Attributive........**kirashimenuru**

g) Future: Conclusive.....**kirashimen, kirashimenan** (I, etc.) shall, or will prob-
Attributive........ or **kirashimuru naran**   ably causet to cut

Oblique—

h) Present Conditional....**kirashimureba**...........as, since, or when (I, etc.)
                causet to cut

i) Past Conditional.......**kirashimeshikaba**.........as, since, or when (I, etc.)
kirashimetareba   caused, etc.,t to cut

j) Present Hypothetical...**kirashimeba**.............if (I, etc.) causet to cut
kirashimenaba
kirashimuru naraba

k) Past Hypothetical......**kirashimetaraba**..........if (I, etc.) caused, etc.,t
kirashimeshi naraba   to cut

l) Optative..............**kirashimebaya**...........Oh! that I could causet to cut

m) Present Actual
Concessive..........**kirashimuredomo**........though (I, etc.) will actually
kirashimu to iedomo   causet to cut

n) Present Hypothetical
Concessive..........**kirashimuru mo**..........even if (I, etc.) causet to
kirashimete mo   cut

o) Past Concessive........**kirashimeshikadomo**......though (I, etc.) caused,
kirashimetaredomo   have, or had causedt to
kirashimetari to iedomo   cut
kirashimeshi to iedomo
kirashimeshi mo

p) Imperative...........**kirashimeyo**..............cause to cut

q) Gerund..............**kirashimete**..............(by) having caused to cut,
                (by) causing to cut

* The sign of the causative is often as (§ 200).
t Some person or thing (§ 206).

FIRST REGULAR CONJUGATION

127. Verb, **kiru**, "to cut," causative affirmative voice—
continued.

POTENTIAL FORMS

Indicative—

a) Indefinite Form........ **kirashimu-beku**

b) Present: Conclusive.... **kirashimu-beshi**..........(I, etc.) will, shall, would,
     Attributive........ **kirashimu-beki**   should, may, might, can,
     could, must, or ought to
     cause* to cut

c) Past: Conclusive....... **kirashimu-bekariki**.......(I, etc.) should, etc., have
     Attributive........ **kirashimu-bekarishi**   caused* to cut

Oblique—

d) Conditional............ **kirashimu-bekereba**......as, or since (I, etc.) should,
     etc., cause* to cut

e) Hypothetical.......... **kirashimu-beku(m)ba**.....if (I, etc.) should, etc.,
     cause* to cut

f) Actual Concessive...... **kirashimu-bekeredomo**....though (I, etc.) should, etc.,
     kirashimu-beshi to iedomo   cause* to cut

g) Hypothetical.......... **kirashimu-beku mo**.......even if (I, etc.) should, etc.,
     cause* to cut

DESIDERATIVE FORMS

Indicative—

h) Indefinite Form........ **kirashime-taku**

i) Present: Conclusive.... **kirashime-tashi**..........(I, etc.) want to cause* to
     Attributive........ **kirashime-taki**   cut

j) Past: Conclusive....... **kirashime-takariki**........(I, etc.) wanted to cause*
     Attributive........ **kirashime-takarishi**   to cut

Oblique—

k) Conditional.......... **kirashime-takereba**.......as, since, or when (I, etc.)
     want to cause* to cut

l) Hypothetical.......... **kirashime-taku(m)ba**.....if (I, etc.) want to cause*
     to cut

m) Concessive........... **kirashime-takeredomo**....though (I, etc.) want to
     kirashime-tashi to iedomo   cause* to cut

ILLATIVE FORMS

Indicative—

n) Past: Conclusive...... **kirashime-keri**...........(I, etc.) caused, have, or
     Attributive........ **kirashime-keru**   had caused* to cut

Oblique—

o) Conditional.......... **kirashime-kereba**.........as, since, or when (I, etc.)
     caused, have, or had
     caused* to cut

p) Concessive........... **kirashime-keredomo**......though (I, etc.) caused, have,
     or had caused* to cut

* Some person or thing (§ 206).

FIRST REGULAR CONJUGATION

128. Verb, **kiru**, "to cut," causative negative voice (stem **kir**, sign of causative **ashim**, remainder of inflection as for second conjugation).

Indicative—

a) Present: Conclusive.... kirashimezu .... (I, you, he, she, it, we, you,
   Attributive........ kirashimezaru .... they) do not cause* to
   kirashimenu   cut
b) Past: Conclusive....... kirashimezariki .... (I, etc.) did not cause, have,
   Attributive........ kirashimezarishi   or had not caused* to cut
c) Future: Conclusive .... kirashimezaru or .... (I, etc.) shall or will not
   kirashimeji   cause* to cut
   Attributive........ kirashimezaran or
   kirashimeji

Oblique—

d) Present Conditional .... kirashimezareba.......... as, since, or when (I, etc.)
   kirashimeneba   do not cause* to cut
e) Past Conditional....... kirashimezarishi-kaba..... as, since, or when (I, etc.)
   kirashimezarishi ni yotte   did not cause, have, or
                                                  had not caused* to cut
f) Present Hypothetical . kirashimezu(m)ba........ if (I,etc.) do not cause* to cut
g) Past Hypothetical..... kirashimezariseba .... if (I, etc.) had not caused*
   kirashimezarishi naraba   to cut
h) Present Actual
   Concessive.......... kirashimezaredomo....... though (I, etc.) do not
   kirashimenedomo   cause* to cut
   kirashimezu to iedomo
i) Present Hypothetical
   Concessive.......... kirashimezaru mo .... even if (I, etc.) do not
                                                  cause* to cut
j) Past Concessive....... kirashimezarishikadomo... though (I, etc.) did not
   kirashimezarishi to iedomo   cause, have, or had not
   kirashimezarishi naredomo   caused* to cut
   kirashimezarishi mo

k) Imperative........... kirashimezare............ cause not, do not cause*
   kirashimuru nakare   to cut
   kirashimuru-na
   kirashimuru koto nakare
l) Gerund.............. kirashimezu.............. (by) not having caused*
   kirashimezu ni   to cut, (by) not causing*
   kirashimezu shite   to cut
   kirashimede

* Some person or thing (§ 206).

[57]

FIRST REGULAR CONJUGATION

129. Verb, **kiru,** "to cut," causative negative voice—*continued.*

POTENTIAL FORMS

Indicative—

a) Indefinite Form........kirashimu-bekarazu
b) Present: Conclusive....kirashimu-bekarazu......(I, etc.) will, shall, would,
　　　Attributive........kirashimu-bekarazaru　　　should, may, might, can,
　　　　　　　　　　　　　　　　　　　　　　　　could, must, or ought not
　　　　　　　　　　　　　　　　　　　　　　　　cause* to cut

c) Past: Conclusive.......kirashimu-bekarazariki....(I, etc.) should not, etc.,
　　　Attributive........kirashimu-bekarazarishi　　have caused* to cut

Oblique—

d) Conditional...........kirashimu-bekarazareba...as, or since (I, etc.) should
　　　　　　　　　　　　　　　　　　　　　　　　not, etc., cause* to cut

e) Hypothetical..........kirashimu-bekarazu(m)ba　if (I, etc.) should not, etc.,
　　　　　　　　　　　　　　　　　　　　　　　　cause* to cut

f) Actual Concessive......kirashimu-bekara-
　　　　　　　　　　　　zaredomo..............though (I, etc.) should not,
　　　　　　　　　　　　kirashimu-bekarazu to　　etc., cause* to cut
　　　　　　　　　　　　iedomo

g) Hypothetical Concessive **kirashimu-bekarazara mo**..even if (I, etc.) should, etc.,
　　　　　　　　　　　　　　　　　　　　　　　　not cause* to cut

PROHIBITIVE FORMS

Indicative—

h) Indefinite Form........kirashimu-majiku
i) Present: Conclusive....kirashimu-maji
　　　Attributive........kirashimu-majiki
j) Past: Conclusive.......kirashimu-majikariki　　Same renderings as for
　　　Attributive........kirashimu-majikarishi　　corresponding Potential
Oblique—　　　　　　　　　　　　　　　　　Forms
k) Conditional...........kirashimu-majikereba
l) Hypothetical..........kirashimu-majiku(m)ba
m) Concessive...........kirashimu-majikeredomo

ILLATIVE FORMS

Indicative—

n) Past: Conclusive......kirashimezari-keri........(I, etc.) did not cause, have
　　　Attributive........kirashimezari-keru　　　not, or had not caused*
　　　　　　　　　　　　　　　　　　　　　　　　to cut

Oblique—

o) Conditional...........kirashimezari-kereba.....as, since, or when (I, etc.)
　　　　　　　　　　　　　　　　　　　　　　　　did not cause, have, or
　　　　　　　　　　　　　　　　　　　　　　　　had not caused* to cut

p) Concessive...........kirashimezari-keredomo...though (I, etc.) did not
　　　　　　　　　　　　　　　　　　　　　　　　cause, have not, or had
　　　　　　　　　　　　　　　　　　　　　　　　not caused* to cut

* Some person and thing (§ 206).

FIRST REGULAR CONJUGATION

130. Verb, **kiru,** "to cut," passive causative affirmative voice*
(stem **kir,** sign of causative **ashim,** of passive **erar,** remainder of
inflections as for second conjugation).

a) Indefinite Form for All
Tenses.............**kirashimerare**

Indicative—
b) Present: Conclusive....**kirashimeraru**............(I, you, he, she, it, we, they)
     Attributive.......**kirashimeraruru**   am, are, or is caused to cut
c) First Past: Conclusive..**kirashimerareki**..........(I, etc.) was, have, or had
     Attributive.......**kirashimerareshi**   been caused to cut
d) Second Past: Conclusive **kirashimeraretari**.........(I, etc.) was, etc., caused to
     Attributive.......**kirashimeraretaru**   cut
e) Third Past: Conclusive **kirashimeraretariki**.......(I, etc.) was, etc., caused to
     Attributive.......**kirashimeraretarishi**   cut
f) Fourth Past: Conclusive **kirashimerarenu**..........(I, etc.) was, etc., caused to
     Attributive.......**kirashimerarenuru**   cut
g) Future Conclusive.....**kirashimeraren**...........(I, etc.) shall or will prob-
      kirashimerarenan   ably be caused to cut
      kirashimeraruru naran

Oblique—
h) Present Conditional....**kirashimerarureba**........as, since, or when (I, etc.)
      am, etc., caused to cut
i) Past Conditional.......**kirashimerareshikaba**.....as, since, or when (I, etc.)
      kirashimeraretareba   was, am caused, have, or
      had been caused to cut
j) Present Hypothetical...**kirashimerareba**..........if (I, etc.) am, etc., caused
      kirashimerarenaba   to cut
      kirashimeraruru naraba
k) Past Hypothetical......**kirashimeraretaraba**......if (I, etc.) had been caused
      kirashimerareshi naraba   to cut
l) Optative.............**kirashimerarebaya**........Oh! that I could be caused
      to cut
m) Present Actual
     Concessive.........**kirashimeraruredomo**.....though (I, etc.) am, etc.,
      kirashimeraru to iedomo   actually caused to cut
n) Present Hypothetical
     Concessive.........**kirashimeraruru mo**......even if (I, etc.) am, etc.,
      kirashimerarete mo   caused to cut
o) Past Concessive.......**kirashimerareshikadomo**..though (I, etc.) was, have
      kirashimeraretaredomo   been, or had been caused
      kirashimeraretari to   to cut
      iedomo
      kirashimerareshi to
      iedomo
      kirashimerareshi mo

p) Imperative...........**kirashimerareyo**..........be caused to cut
q) Gerund..............**kirashimerarete**..........(by) having been caused to
      cut, (by) being caused to
      cut

r) * The form **kiraseraruru** is also seen (§ 201).

FIRST REGULAR CONJUGATION

131. Verb, **kiru,** "to cut," passive causative affirmative voice
—*continued.*

POTENTIAL FORMS

Indicative—
a) Indefinite Form........**kirashimeraru-beku**
b) Present: Conclusive ...**kirashimeraru-beshi**......(I, etc.) will, shall, would,
         Attributive........**kirashimeraru-beki**   should, may, might, can,
                                                        could, must, or ought to
                                                        be caused to cut

c) Past: Conclusive......**kirashimeraru-bekariki** ...(I, etc.) should, etc., have
         Attributive........**kirashimeraru-bekarishi**   been caused to cut

Oblique—
d) Conditional..........**kirashimeraru-bekereba** .. as, or since (I, etc.) should,
                                                        etc., be caused to cut

e) Hypothetical.........**kirashimeraru-beku(m)ba** if (I, etc.) should, etc., be
                                                        caused to cut

f) Actual Concessive.....**kirashimeraru-**
                       bekeredomo..........though (I, etc.) should, etc.,
                       kirashimeraru-beshi to   be caused to cut
                       iedomo

g) Hypothetical Concessive **kirashimeraru-beku mo** ...even if (I, etc.) should, etc.,
                                                        be caused to cut

DESIDERATIVE FORMS

Indicative—
h) Indefinite Form........**kirashimerare-taku**
i) Present: Conclusive....**kirashimerare-tashi**.......(I, etc.) want to be caused
         Attributive.......**kirashimerare-taki**   to cut
j) Past: Conclusive......**kirashimerare-takariki**... (I, etc.) wanted to be
         Attributive.......**kirashimerare-takarishi**   caused to cut

Oblique—
k) Conditional..........**kirashimerare-takereba**...as, since, or when (I, etc.)
                                                        want to be caused to cut

l) Hypothetical.........**kirashimerare-taku(m)ba**..if (I, etc.) want to be
                                                        caused to cut

m) Concessive..........**kirashimerare-takeredomo** though (I, etc.) want to be
                       kirashimerare-tashi to   caused to cut
                       iedomo

ILLATIVE FORMS

Indicative—
n) Past: Conclusive......**kirashimerare-keri**.......(I, etc.) was caused, have,
         Attributive........**kirashimerare-keru**   or had been caused to cut

Oblique—
o) Conditional..........**kirashimerare-kereba**.....as, since, or when (I, etc.)
                                                        was caused, have, or had
                                                        been caused to cut

p) Concessive..........**kirashimerare-keredomo**.. though (I, etc.) was, have,
                                                        or had been caused to cut

FIRST REGULAR CONJUGATION

132. Verb, **kiru**, "to cut," passive causative negative voice (stem **kir**, sign of causative **ashim**, of passive **erar**, remainder of inflections as for second conjugation).

Indicative—

a) Present: Conclusive.... kirashimerarezu..........(I, you, he, she, it, we, they)
   Attributive........ kirashimerarezaru   am, are, or is not caused
                       kirashimerarenu   to cut
b) Past: Conclusive....... kirashimerarezariki.......(I, etc.) was not caused,
   Attributive........ kirashimerarezarishi   have not, or had not been
                                                      caused to cut
c) Future: Conclusive.... kirashimerarezaru or
                       kirashimerareji.........(I, etc.) shall or will not be
   Attributive........ kirashimerarezaran or   caused to cut
                       kirashimerareji

Oblique—

d) Present Conditional.... kirashimerarezareba......as, since, or when (I, etc.)
                       kirashimerareneba   am, etc., not caused to cut
e) Past Conditional....... kirashimerarezari-shikaba as, since, or when (I, etc.)
                       kirashimerarezarishi ni   was not caused, have, or
                       yotte   had not been caused to
                                                  cut
f) Present Hypothetical... kirashimerarezu(m)ba....if (I, etc.) am, etc., not
                                                   caused to cut
g) Past Hypothetical...... kirashimerarezariseba.....if (I, etc.) had not been
                       kirashimerarezarishi   caused to cut
                       naraba
h) Present Actual
   Concessive......... kirashimerarezaredomo...though (I, etc.) am, etc.,
                       kirashimerarenedomo   not caused to cut
                       kirashimerarezu to iedomo
i) Present Hypothetical
   Concessive......... kirashimerarezaru mo.....even if (I, etc.) am, etc.,
                                                not caused to cut
j) Past Concessive....... kirashimerarezarishi-
                       kadomo..............though (I, etc.) was not
                       kirashimerarezarishi to   caused, have, or had not
                       iedomo   been caused to cut
                       kirashimerarezarishi-
                       naredomo
                       kirashimerarezarishi mo
___
k) Imperative........... kirashimerarezare........be not caused to cut
                       kirashimeraruru nakare
                       kirashimeraruru-na
                       kirashimeraruru koto
                       nakare
l) Gerund.............. kirashimerarezu.........(by) not having been caused
                       kirashimerarezu ni   to cut, (by) not being
                       kirashimerarezu shite   caused to cut
                       kirashimerarede

[61]

FIRST REGULAR CONJUGATION

133. Verb, **kiru,** "to cut," passive causative negative **voice—**
continued.

POTENTIAL FORMS

Indicative—
a) Indefinite Form........kirashimeraru-bekarazu
b) Present: Conclusive....kirashimeraru-bekarazu...(I, etc.) will, shall, would,
     Attributive........kirashimeraru-bekarazaru should, may, might, can,
                            could, must, or ought
c) Past: Conclusive......kirashimeraru-   not to be caused to cut
                 bekarazariki...........(I, etc.) should not, etc.,
     Attributive........kirashimeraru-   have been caused to cut
Oblique—   bekarazarishi
d) Conditional..........kirashimeraru-
                 bekarazareba..........as, or since (I, etc.) should
                            not, etc., have been
e) Hypothetical..........kirashimeraru-   caused to cut
                 bekarazu(m)ba ....if (I, etc.) should not, etc.,
f) Actual Concessive......kirashimeraru-bekarazare- have been caused to cut
                 domo.................though (I, etc.) should not,
                 kirashimeraru-bekarazu etc., have been caused to
                 to iedomo   cut
g) Hypothetical Concessive kirashimeraru-bekarazaru
                 mo..................even if (I, etc.) should, etc.,
                            not have been caused to
                            cut

PROHIBITIVE FORMS

Indicative—
h) Indefinite Form........kirashimeraru-majiku
i) Present: Conclusive....kirashimeraru-maji
     Attributive........kirashimeraru-majiki
j) Past: Conclusive......kirashimeraru-majikariki
     Attributive........kirashimeraru-
Oblique—   majikarishi   Same renderings as for
k) Conditional..........kirashimeraru-   corresponding Potential
                 majikereba   Forms
l) Hypothetical.........kirashimeraru-
                 majiku(m)ba
m) Concessive..........kirashimeraru-
                 majikeredomo

ILLATIVE FORMS

Indicative—
n) Past: Conclusive......kirashimerarezari-keri....(I, etc.) was not caused,
     Attributive........kirashimerarezari-keru have, or had not been
Oblique—   caused to cut
o) Conditional..........kirashimerarezari-kereba..as, since. or when (I, etc.)
                              was not caused, have, or
p) Concessive..........kirashimerarezari-   had not been caused to cut
                 keredomo.............though (I, etc.) was not
                            caused, have, or had not
                            been caused to cut

SECOND REGULAR CONJUGATION

134. Verb, **homuru,** "to praise" (stem **hom**), active affirmative voice.

a) Indefinite Form for All
Tenses..............**home**

Indicative—
b) Present: Conclusive....**homu**..................(I, you, he, she, it, we, they)
Attributive........**homuru**   praise
c) First Past: Conclusive..**homeki**.................(I, etc.) praised, have, or
Attributive........**homeshi**   had praised
d) Second Past: Conclusive **hometari**...............(I, etc.) praised, have, or
Attributive........**hometaru**   had praised
e) Third Past: Conclusive..**hometariki**..............(I, etc.) praised, have, or
Attributive........**hometarishi**   had praised
f) Fourth Past: Conclusive **homenu**.................(I, etc.) praised, have, or
Attributive........**homenuru***   had praised
g) Future: Conclusive....**homen, homenan,** or
Attributive........ **homuru naran**..........(I, etc.) shall or will probably praise

Oblique—
h) Present Conditional....**homureba**...............as, since, or when (I, etc.) praise
i) Past Conditional.......**homeshikaba**............as, since, or when (I, etc.)
hometareba   praised, have, or had praised
j) Present Hypothetical...**homeba**................if (I, etc.) praise
homenaba
homuru naraba
k) Past Hypothetical......**hometaraba**.............if (I, etc.) had praised
homeshi naraba
l) Optative.............**homebaya**..............Oh that I could praise!
m) Present Actual
Concessive.........**homuredomo**...........though (I, etc.) do actually
homu to iedomo   praise
n) Present Hypothetical
Concessive.........**homuru mo**.............even if (I, etc.) praise
homete mo
o) Past Concessive.......**homeshikadomo**.........though (I, etc.) praised,
hometaredomo   have praised, or had
hometari to iedomo   praised
homeshi to iedomo
homeshi mo

---

p) Imperative...........**homeyo**................praise
q) Gerund..............**homete**................(by) having praised, (by) praising

· Sometimes **hometsuru**.

[63]

SECOND REGULAR CONJUGATION

135. Verb, **homuru**, "to praise" (stem **hom**), active affirmative voice—*continued.*

POTENTIAL FORMS

Indicative—

a) Indefinite Form........**homu-beku**

b) Present: Conclusive....**homu-beshi**..............(I, etc.) will, shall, would,

       Attributive........**homu-beki**   should, may, might, can,
                                         could, must, or ought to
                                       praise

c) Past: Conclusive.......**homu-bekariki**...........(I, etc.) should, etc., have

       Attributive........**homu-bekarishi**   praised

Oblique—

d) Conditional...........**homu-bekereba**..........as, or since (I, etc.) should,
                                       etc., praise

e) Hypothetical.........**homu-beku(m)ba**........if (I, etc.) should, etc.,
                                       praise

f) Actual Concessive......**homu-bekeredomo**.......though (I, etc.) should, etc.,
               homu-beshi to iedomo   praise

g) Hypothetical Concessive **homu-beku mo**...........even if (I, etc.) should, etc.,
                                         praise

DESIDERATIVE FORMS

Indicative—

h) Indefinite Form........**home-taku**

i) Present: Conclusive....**home-tashi**..............(I, etc.) want to praise

       Attributive........**home-taki**

j) Past: Conclusive.......**home-takariki**............(I, etc.) wanted to praise

       Attributive........**home-takarishi**

Oblique—

k) Conditional...........**home-takereba**...........as, since, or when (I, etc.)
                                       want to praise

l) Hypothetical.........**home-taku(m)ba**........if (I, etc.) want to praise

m) Concessive...........**home-takeredomo**.......though (I, etc.) want to
               home-tashi to iedomo   praise

ILLATIVE FORMS

Indicative—

n) Past: Conclusive.......**home-keri**...............(I, etc.) praised, have, or

       Attributive........**home-keru**   had praised

Oblique—

o) Conditional..........**home-kereba**.............as, since, or when (I, etc.)
                                       praised, have, or had
                                       praised

p) Concessive...........**home-keredomo**..........though, (I, etc.) praised,
                                       have, or had praised

SECOND REGULAR CONJUGATION

136. Verb, **homuru,** "to praise" (stem **hom**), active negative voice.

Indicative—
a) Present: Conclusive....**homezu**................(I, you, he, she, it, we, they)
       Attributive........**homenu**   do not praise
                    homezaru
b) Past: Conclusive.......**homezariki**...............(I, etc.) did not praise,
       Attributive........**homezarishi**   have not, or had not praised
c) Future: Conclusive.....**homezaru** or **homeji**......(I, etc.) shall or will not
       Attributive........**homezaran** or **homeji**   praise
Oblique—
d) Present Conditional....**homezareba**.............as, since, or when (I, etc.)
                   homeneba   do not praise
e) Past Conditional.......**homezarishikaba**.........as, since, or when (I, etc.)
                   homezarishi ni yotte   do not praise, have not, or had not praised
f) Present Hypothetical...**homezu(m)ba**...........if (I, etc.) do not praise
g) Past Hypothetical......**homezariseba**...........if (I, etc.) had not praised
                   homezarishi naraba
h) Present Actual
    Concessive.........**homezaredomo**...........though (I, etc.) do not
                   homenedomo   praise
                   homezu to iedomo
i) Present Hypothetical
    Concessive.........**homezaru mo**...........even if (I, etc.) do not praise
j) Past Concessive........**homezarishikadomo**.......though (I, etc.) did not
                   homezarishi to iedomo   praise, have not, or had
                   homezarishi naredomo   not praised
                   homezarishi mo

k) Imperative...........**homezare**...............praise not, do not praise
                   homuru nakare
                   homuru-na
                   homuru koto nakare
l) Gerund..............**homezu**................(by) not having praised,
                   homezu ni   (by) not praising
                   homezu shite
                   homede
m) Causative Negative
    Form.............**homezarashimuru** (§ 204)..(I, etc.) cause (someone) not to praise

SECOND REGULAR CONJUGATION

137. Verb, **homuru,** "to praise" (stem **hom**), active negative voice—*continued.*

POTENTIAL FORMS

Indicative—
a) Indefinite Form........homu-bekarazu
b) Present: Conclusive....homu-bekarazu..........(I, etc.) will, shall, would,
    Attributive.......homu-bekarazaru   should, may, might, can,
                                                     could, must, or ought not
                                                     to praise
c) Past: Conclusive......homu-bekarazariki.......(I, etc.) should, etc., not
         homu-bekarazarishi   have praised

Oblique—
d) Conditional...........homu-bekarazareba.......as, or since (I, etc.) should,
                                                     etc., not praise
e) Hypothetical..........homu-bekarazu(m)ba.....if (I, etc.) should, etc., not
                                                     praise
f) Actual Concessive......homu-bekarazaredomo....though (I, etc.) should, etc.,
         homu-bekarazu to iedomo   not praise
g) Hypothetical Concessive homu-bekarazaru mo.....even if (I, etc.) should, etc.,
                                                     not praise

PROHIBITIVE FORMS

Indicative—
h) Indefinite Form........homu-majiku
i) Present: Conclusive....homu-maji
    Attributive........homu-majiki
j) Past: Conclusive......homu-majikariki
    Attributive........homu-majikarishi   } Same renderings as for
Oblique—   corresponding Potential
k) Conditional...........homu-majikereba   Forms
l) Hypothetical..........homu-majiku(m)ba
m) Concessive............homu-najikeredomo   }

ILLATIVE FORMS

Indicative—
n) Past: Conclusive......homezari-keri............(I, etc.) did not praise,
    Attributive........homezari-keru   have, or had not praised
Oblique—
o) Conditional...........homezari-kereba.........as, since, or when (I, etc.)
                                                     did not praise, have not,
                                                     or had not praised
p) Concessive............homezari-keredomo.......though (I, etc.) did not
                                                     praise, have not, or had
                                                     not praised

---

q) Passive...............homeraruru, etc., see §§ 122 and 189
   Causative.............homeshimuru or homesasuru, see §§ 126, 199, 200
   Passive Causative......homeshimeraruru or
                          homesaseraruru, etc., see §§ 130 and 201

THIRD REGULAR CONJUGATION

138. Verb, **suguru,** "to pass" (stem **sug**), active affirmative voice.

a) Indefinite Form for All
Tenses.............**sugi**

Indicative—

b) Present: Conclusive....**sugu**...................(I, you, he, she, it, we, they)
Attributive........**suguru**   pass

c) First Past: Conclusive..**sugiki**..................(I, etc.) passed, have, or
Attributive.......**sugishi**   had passed

d) Second Past: Conclusive **sugitari**................(I, etc.) passed, have, or
Attributive........**sugitaru**   had passed

e) Third Past: Conclusive...**sugitariki**..............(I, etc.) passed, have, or
Attributive........**sugitarishi**   had passed

f) Fourth Past: Conclusive **suginu**.................(I, etc.) passed, have, or
Attributive.......**suginuru**   had passed away

g) Future: Conclusive....**sugin, suginan** or.........(I, etc.) shall or will prob-
Attributive.......**suguru naran**   ably pass

Oblique—

h) Present Conditional....**sugureba**...............as, since, or when (I, etc.)
                                              pass

i) Past Conditional.......**sugishikaba**..............(I, etc.) pass, have, or had
sugitareba   passed

j) Present Hypothetical...**sugiba**.................if (I, etc.) pass
suginaba
suguru naraba

k) Past Hypothetical......**sugitaraba**..............if (I, etc.) had passed
sugishi naraba

l) Optative.............**sugibaya**................Oh that I could pass!

m) Present Actual
Concessive.........**suguredomo**............though (I, etc.) do actually
sugu to iedomo   pass

n) Present Hypothetical
Concessive.........**suguru mo** ....even if (I, etc.) pass
sugite mo

o) Past Concessive.......**sugishikadomo** ....though (I, etc.) passed,
sugitaredomo   have, or had passed
sugitari to iedomo
sugishi to iedomo
sugishi mo

---

p) Imperative...........**sugiyo**..................pass!

q) Gerund..............**sugite**..................(by) having passed, (by)
                                              passing

THIRD REGULAR CONJUGATION

139. Verb, **suguru,** "to pass" (stem **sug**), active affirmative voice—*continued.*

POTENTIAL FORMS

Indicative—

a) Indefinite Form........ sugu-beku

b) Present: Conclusive.... sugu-beshi..............(I, etc.) will, shall, would,
   Attributive........ sugu-beki   should, may. might, can
                could, must, or ought to
                pass

c) Past: Conclusive....... sugu-bekariki............(I, etc.) should, etc., have
   Attributive........ sugu-bekarishi   passed

Oblique—

d) Conditional.......... sugu-bekereba...........as, or since (I, etc.) should,
                etc., pass

e) Hypothetical.......... sugu-beku(m)ba..........if (I, etc.) should, etc., pass

f) Actual Concessive...... sugu-bekeredomo.......though (I, etc.) should, etc.,
       sugu-beshi to iedomo pass

g) Hypothetical Concessive sugu-beku mo...........even if (I, etc.) should, etc.,
                pass

DESIDERATIVE FORMS

Indicative—

h) Indefinite Form........ **sugi-taku**

i) Present: Conclusive.... **sugi-tashi**..............(I, etc.) want to pass
   Attributive........ **sugi-taki**

j) Past: Conclusive....... **sugi-takariki**.............(I, etc.) wanted to pass
   Attributive........ **sugi-takarishi**

Oblique—

k) Conditional.......... **sugi-takereba**...........as, since, or when (I, etc.)
                want to pass

l) Hypothetical.......... **sugi-taku(m)ba**..........if (I, etc.) want to pass

m) Concessive.......... **sugi-takeredomo**........though (I, etc.) want to
       sugi-tashi to iedomo pass

ILLATIVE FORMS

Indicative—

n) Past: Conclusive....... **sugi-keri**...............(I, etc.) passed, have, or
   Attributive........ **sugi-keru**   had passed

Oblique—

o) Conditional.......... **sugi-kereba**.............as, since, or when (I, etc.)
                passed, have, or had
                passed

p) Concessive.......... **sugi-keredomo**...........though (I, etc.) passed,
                have, or had passed

THIRD REGULAR CONJUGATION

140. Verb, **suguru,** "to pass" (stem **sug**), active negative voice.

Indicative—

a) Present: Conclusive.... **sugizu**................(I, you, he, she, it, we, you
       Attributive........ **sugizaru**   they) do not pass
                  suginu

b) Past: Conclusive....... **sugizariki**................(I, etc.) did not pass, have
       Attributive........ **sugizarishi**   or had not passed

c) Future: Conclusive..... **sugizaran or sugiji**........(I, etc.) shall not pass
       Attributive........ **sugizaran or sugiji**

Oblique—

d) Present Conditional.... **sugizareba**...............as, since, or when (I, etc.)
                 sugineba   do not pass

e) Past Conditional....... **sugizarishikaba**..........as, since. or when (I, etc.)
                 sugizarishi ni yotte   did not, have not, or had
                                     not passed

f) Present Hypothetical... **sugizu(m)ba**.............if (I, etc.) do not pass

g) Past Hypothetical...... **sugizariseba**.............if (I, etc.) had not passed
                 sugizarishi naraba

h) Present Actual
       Concessive......... **sugizaredomo**...........though (I, etc.) do not pass
                 suginedomo
                 sugizu to iedomo

i) Present Hypothetical
       Concessive......... **sugizaru mo**..............even if (I, etc.) do not pass

j) Past Concessive....... **sugizarishikadomo**........though (I, etc.) did not pass,
                 sugizarishi to iedomo   have or had not passed
                 sugizarishi naredomo
                 sugizarishi mo

---

k) Imperative........... **sugizare**................pass not, do not pass!
                 suguru nakare
                 suguru-na
                 suguru koto nakare

l) Gerund.............. **sugizu**..................(by) not having passed.
                 sugizu ni   (by) not passing
                 sugizu shite
                 sugide

m) Causative Negative .... **sugizarashimuru** (§ 204)....(I, etc.) cause (someone)
                                             not to pass

THIRD REGULAR CONJUGATION

141. Verb, **suguru,** "to pass" (stem **sug**), active negative voice—*continued.*

POTENTIAL FORMS

Indicative—
a) Indefinite Form........**sugu-bekarazu**
b) Present: Conclusive....**sugu-bekarazu**...........(I, etc.) will, shall, would,
 Attributive........**sugu-bekarazaru**   should. may, might, can,
                                                       could, must, or ought
                                                       not to pass

Oblique—
c) Past: Conclusive......**sugu-bekarazariki**........(I, etc.) should, etc., not
 Attributive........**sugu-bekarazarishi**   have passed
d) Conditional...........**sugu-bekarazareba**.......as, or since (I, etc.) should,
                                                      etc., not pass
e) Hypothetical..........**sugu-bekarazu(m)ba**......if (I, etc.) should, etc. not
                                                      pass
f) Actual Concessive......**sugu-bekarazaredomo**.....though (I, etc.) should, etc.,
    sugu-bekarazu to iedomo   not pass
g) Hypothetical Concessive **sugu-bekarazaru mo**......even if (I, etc.) should, etc.,
                                                       not pass

PROHIBITIVE FORMS

Indicative—
h) Indefinite Form ....**sugu-majiku**
i) Present: Conclusive....**sugu-maji**
 Attributive.......**sugu-majiki**
j) Past: Conclusive......**sugu-majikariki**   Same renderings as for
 Attributive........**sugu-majikarishi**   corresponding Potential
Oblique—   Forms
k) Conditional...........**sugu-majikereba**
l) Hypothetical..........**sugu-majiku(m)ba**
m) Concessive...........**sugu-majikeredomo**

ILLATIVE FORMS

Indicative—
n) Past: Conclusive......**sugizari-keri**.............(I, etc.) did not pass, have
 Attributive........**sugizari-keru**   or had not passed
Oblique—
o) Conditional...........**sugizari-kereba**...........as, since, or when (I, etc.)
                                                       did not pass, have not,
                                                       or had not passed
p) Concessive...........**sugizari-keredomo**........though (I, etc.) did not
                                                      pass, have, or had not
                                                      passed

_____

q) Passive...............**sugiraruru**...............See §§ 122 and 189
 Causative............**sugishimuru or sugisasuru** See §§ 126, 199, 200
 Passive Causative......**sugishimeraruru or**
             sugisaseraruru.........See §§ 130 and 201

FOURTH REGULAR CONJUGATION

142. Verb, **miru,** "to see" (stem **mi**), active affirmative voice
—*continued.*

a) Indefinite Form of All
    Tenses..............**mi**

Indicative—

b) Present: Conclusive....**miru**...................(I, you, he, she, it. you,
    Attributive.......**miru**   they), see, sees
c) First Past: Conclusive..**miki**...................(I, etc.) saw, have, or had
    Attributive........**mishi**   seen
d) Second Past: Conclusive **mitari**..................(I, etc.) saw, have, or had
    Attributive........**mitaru**   seen
e) Third Past: Conclusive..**mitariki**................(I, etc.) saw, have, or had
    Attributive........**mitarishi**   seen
f) Fourth Past: Conclusive **mitsu***.................(I, etc.) saw, have, or had
    Attributive........**mitsuru***   seen
g) Future Conclusive.....**min** or **miru naran**........(I, etc.) shall or will prob-
             ably see

Oblique—

h) Present Conditional....**mireba**.................as, since, or when (I, etc.)
             see
i) Past Conditional.......**mishikaba**...............as, since, or when (I, etc.)
    mitareba   saw, have or had seen
j) Present Hypothetical...**miba**...................if (I, etc.) see
    minaba
    miru naraba
k) Past Hypothetical......**mitaraba**...............if (I, etc.) had seen
    mishi naraba
l) Optative.............**mibaya**.................oh that I could see!
m) Present Actual
    Concessive.........**miru mo**................even if (I, etc.) see
    mite mo
n) Past Concessive.......**mishikadomo**............though (I, etc.) saw, have,
    mitaredomo   or had seen
    mitari to iedomo
    mishi to iedomo
    mishi mo

---

o) Imperative...........**miyo**...................see!
p) Gerund..............**mite**...................(by) having seen, (by)
            seeing

* The only other verbs possessing this fourth past are **kiru**, "to wear," **miru**, "to boil," and **niru**, "to resemble."

FOURTH REGULAR CONJUGATION

143. Verb, **miru**, "to see" (stem **mi**), active affirmative voice—*continued.*

POTENTIAL FORMS

Indicative—

a) Indefinite Form........**mi(ru)-beku**

b) Present: Conclusive ....**mi(ru)-beshi**.............(I, etc.) will, shall, would,
   Attributive........**mi(ru)-beki**   should, may, might, can,
                                              could, must, or ought to
                                              see

c) Past: Conclusive......**mi(ru)-bekariki**...........(I, etc.) should, etc., have
   Attributive....... **mi(ru)-bekarishi**   seen

Oblique—

d) Conditional...........**mi(ru)-bekereba**..........as, or since (I, etc.) should,
                                                    etc., see

e) Hypothetical..........**mi(ru)-beku(m)ba**........if (I, etc.) should, etc., see

f) Actual Concessive......**mi(ru)-bekeredomo**.......though (I, etc.) should, etc.,
      mi(ru)-beshi to iedomo   see

g) Hypothetical Concessive **mi(ru)-beku mo**..........even if (I, etc.) should, etc.,
                                                    see

DESIDERATIVE FORMS

Indicative—

h) Indefinite Form........**mi-taku**

i) Present: Conclusive ....**mi-tashi**.................(I, etc.) want to see
   Attributive........**mi-taki**

j) Past: Conclusive......**mi-takariki**..............(I, etc.) wanted to see
   Attributive........**mi-takarishi**

Oblique—

k) Conditional...........**mi-takereba**.............as, since, or when (I, etc.)
                                                    want to see

l) Hypothetical..........**mi-taku(m)ba**............if (I, etc.) want to see

m) Concessive...........**mitakeredomo**...........though (I, etc.) want to see
      mi-tashi to iedomo

ILLATIVE FORMS

Indicative—

n) Past: Conclusive.......**mi-keri**.................(I, etc.) saw, have, or had
   Attributive........**mi-keru**   seen

Oblique—

o) Conditional...........**mi-kereba**..............as, since, or when (I, etc.)
                                                    saw, have, or had seen

p) Concessive...........**mi-keredomo**...........though (I, etc.) saw, have,
                                                    or had seen

FOURTH REGULAR CONJUGATION

144. Verb, miru, "to see" (stem mi), active negative voice.

Indicative—

a) Present: Conclusive.... **mizu**....................(I, you, he, she, it, we, you,
   Attributive........ **mizaru**   they) do, does not see
b) Past: Conclusive....... **mizariki**.................(I, etc.) did not see, have,
   Attributive........ **mizarishi**   or had not seen
c) Future: Conclusive..... **mizaran or miji**..........(I, etc.) shall or will not see
   Attributive........ **mizaran or miji**

Oblique—

d) Present Conditional.... **mizareba**...............as, since, or when (I, etc.)
   mineba   do not see
e) Past Conditional....... **mizarishikaba**...........as, since, or when (I, etc.)
   mizarishi ni yotte   did not see, have, or had
                           not seen
f) Present Hypothetical... **mizu(m)ba**..............if (I, etc.) do not see
g) Past Hypothetical...... **mizariseba**..............if (I, etc) had not seen
   mizarishi naraba
h) Present Actual
   Concessive......... **mizaredomo**............though (I, etc.) do not see
   minedomo
   mizu to iedomo
i) Present Hypothetical
   Concessive......... **mizaru mo**...............even if (I, etc.) do not see
j) Past Concessive....... **mizarishikadomo**........though (I, etc.) did not see,
   mizarishi to iedomo   have, or had not seen
   mizarishi naredomo
   mizarishi mo

---

k) Imperative........... **mizare**.................see not, do not see!
   miru nakare
   miru-na
   miru koto nakare
l) Gerund.............. **mizu**....................(by) not having seen, (by)
   mizu ni   not seeing
   mizu shite
   mide
m) Causative Negative..... **mizarashimuru** (§ 204)....(I, etc.) cause (someone)
                           not to see

FOURTH REGULAR CONJUGATION

145. Verb, **miru**, "to see" (stem **mi**), active negative voice—
continued.

POTENTIAL FORMS

Indicative—
a) Indefinite Form........mi(ru)-bekarazu
b) Present: Conclusive....mi(ru)-bekarazu.........(I, etc.) will, shall, would,
    Attributive........mi(ru)-bekarazaru   should, may, might, can,
    could, must, or ought
    not to see
c) Past: Conclusive.......mi(ru)-bekarazariki.......(I, etc.) should, etc., not
    Attributive........mi(ru)-bekarazarishi   have seen
Oblique—
d) Conditional...........mi(ru)-bekarazareba......as, or since (I, etc.) should,
    etc., not see
e) Hypothetical..........mi(ru)-bekarazu(m)ba....if (I, etc.) should, etc., not see
f) Actual Concessive......mi(ru)-bekarazaredomo...though (I, etc.) should, etc.,
    mi(ru)-bekarazu to iedomo   not see
g) Hypothetical Concessive mi(ru)-bekarazarumo.....even if (I, etc.) should, etc.,
    not see

PROHIBITIVE FORMS

Indicative—
h) Indefinite Form........mi(ru)majiku
i) Present: Conclusive....mi(ru)-maji
    Attributive.......mi(ru)-majiki
j) Past: Conclusive......mi(ru)-majikariki
    Attributive.......mi(ru)-maji karishi
Oblique—
k) Conditional...........mi(ru)-majikereba
l) Hypothetical..........mi(ru)-majiku(m)ba
m) Concessive...........mi(ru)-majikeredomo

Same renderings as for corresponding Potential Forms

ILLATIVE FORMS

Indicative—
n) Past: Conclusive.......mizari-keri..............(I, etc.) did not see, have
    Attributive........mizari-keru   or had not seen
Oblique—
o) Conditional...........mizari-kereba...........as, since, or when (I, etc.)
    did not see, have, or had
    not seen
p) Concessive...........mizari-keredomo........though (I, etc.) did not see,
    have, or had not seen

q) Passive Form.........miraruru................See §§ 122 and 189
    Causative Form.......miseshimuru or misasuru .See §§ 126 199, 200
    Passive Causative Form miseshimeraruru or
        misaseraruru..........See §§ 130 and 201

IRREGULAR VERB **SURU**,* "TO DO" (STEM **S**)

146. Active affirmative voice.

a) Indefinite Form for All
      Tenses . . . . **shi**

Indicative—

b) Present: Conclusive . . . . **su** . . . . (I, you, he, she, it, we, you,
      Attributive . . . . **suru**   they) do

c) Perfect: Conclusive . . . . **seri** . . . . (I, etc.) did, have, or had
      Attributive . . . . **seru**   done

d) First Past: Conclusive . . **shiki** . . . . (I, etc.) did, have, or had
      Attributive . . . . **seshi**   done

e) Second Past: Conclusive **shitari** . . . . (I, etc.) did, have, or had
      Attributive . . . . **shitaru**   done

f) Third Past: Conclusive . . **shitariki** . . . . (I, etc.) did, have. or had
      Attributive . . . . **shitarishi**   done

g) Fourth Past: Conclusive **shinu** . . . . (I, etc.) did, have, or had
      Attributive . . . . **shinuru**   done entirely

h) Future Conclusive or . . . **sen** or **shinan** . . . . (I, etc.) shall, will, probably
      Attributive   do, am about to do

Oblique—

i) Present Conditional . . . . **sureba** . . . . as, since, or when (I, etc.) do

j) Past Conditional . . . . **seshikaba** . . . . as, since, or when (I, etc.)
      shitareba   did, have, or had done

k) Present Hypothetical . . . **seba** . . . . if (I, etc.) do
      senaba

l) Past Hypothetical . . . . . . **shitaraba** . . . . if (I, etc.) had done
      seshi naraba

m) Optative . . . . **sebaya** . . . . Oh, that I could do!

n) Present Actual
      Concessive . . . . **suredomo** . . . . though (I, etc.) do actually
      su to iedomo   do

o) Present Hypothetical
      Concessive . . . . **suru mo** . . . . even if (I, etc.) do
      shite mo

p) Past Concessive . . . . **seshikadomo** . . . . though (I, etc.) did, have,
      shitaredomo   or had done
      shitari to iedomo
      shitarumo
      seshi mo

---

q) Imperative . . . . **seyo** . . . . do!

r) Gerund . . . . **shite** . . . . (by) having done (by) doing

* Generally used in combination with nouns (see § 221*b*). In this use the English verbal translation can be secured by inserting the verb in place of "do," "did," or "done" above. See also to **suru**, § 169.

IRREGULAR VERB SURU. "TO DO" (STEM S)

147. Active affirmative voice—*continued.*

POTENTIAL FORMS

Indicative—
a) Indefinite Form........**su-beku**
b) Present: Conclusive....**su-beshi**.................(I, etc.) will, shall, would
    Attributive........**su-beki**   should, may, might, can
                               could, must, or ought to do
c) Past: Conclusive.......**su-bekariki**..............(I. etc.) should, etc., have
    Attributive........**su-bekarishi**   done
Oblique—
d) Conditional...........**su-bekereba**............as, or since (I, etc.) should,
                              etc., do
e) Hypothetical..........**su-beku(m)ba**...........if (I. etc.) should, etc., do
f) Actual Concessive......**su-bekeredomo**..........though (I. etc.) should, etc.,
           su-beshi to iedomo   do
g) Hypothetical Concessive **su-beku mo**.............even if (I, etc.) should, etc.,
                              do

DESIDERATIVE FORMS

Indicative—
h) Indefinite Form........**shi-taku**
i) Present: Conclusive....**shi-tashi**.................(I, etc.) want to do
    Attributive.......**shi-tak**
j) Past: Conclusive.......**shi-takariki**..............(I, etc.) wanted to do
    Attributive........**shi-takarishi**
Oblique—
k) Conditional...........**shi-takereba**............as, since, or when (I, etc.)
                              want to do
) Hypothetical..........**shi-taku(m)ba**...........if (I, etc.) want to do
m) Concessive...........**shi-takeredomo**..........though (I, etc.) want to do
           shi-tashi to iedomo

ILLATIVE FORMS

Indicative—
n) Past: Conclusive.......**shi-keri**.................(I, etc.) did, have, or had
    Attributive........**shi-keru**   done
Oblique—
o) Conditional...........**shi-kereba**...............as, since, or when (I, etc.)
                              did, have, or had done
p) Concessive...........**shi-keredomo**...........though (I, etc.) did, have,
                              or had done

IRREGULAR VERB **SURU**, "TO DO" (STEM **S**)

148. Active negative voice.

Indicative—
a) Present: Conclusive.... **sezu, sezaru** .... (I, you, he, she, it, we, they)
   Attributive........ **senu**   do not do
b) Past: Conclusive....... **sezariki** .... (I, etc.) did not do, have, or
   Attributive........ **sezarishi**   had not done
c) Future: Conclusive..... **sezaran** .... (I, etc.) shall or will not do
   Attributive........ **sezaran**

Oblique—
d) Present Conditional.... **sezareba** .... as, since, or when (I, etc.)
   seneba   do not do
e) Past Conditional....... **sezarishikaba** .... as, since, or when (I, etc.)
   sezarishi ni yotte   did not do, have, or had
   sezarishi tame   not done
f) Present Hypothetical... **sezu(m)ba** .... if (I, etc.) do not do
g) Past Hypothetical...... **sezariseba** .... if (I, etc.) had not done
   sezarishi naraba
h) Present Actual
   Concessive.......... **sezaredomo** .... though (I, etc.) do not do
   senedomo
   sezu to iedomo
i) Present Hypothetical
   Concessive.......... **sezaru mo** .... even if (I, etc.) do not do
j) Past Concessive....... **sezarishikadomo** .... though (I, etc.) did not do
   sezarishi to iedomo   have, or had not done
   sezarishi naredomo
   sezarishi mo

k) Imperative........... **sezare** .... do not, do not do!
   suru nakare
   suru-na
   su-na
l) Gerund............. **sezu** .... (by) not having done, (by)
   sezu ni   not doing
   sezu shite
   sede

IRREGULAR VERB SURU, "TO DO" (STEM S)

149. Active negative voice—*continued.*

POTENTIAL FORMS

Indicative—
a) Indefinite Form........su-bekarazu
b) Present: Conclusive....su-bekarazu.............(I, etc.) will, shall, would
   Attributive........su-bekarazaru   should, may, might, can,
                                             could, must, or ought
                                             not to do
c) Past: Conclusive......su-bekarazariki..........(I, etc.) should etc., not
   Attributive........su-bekarazarishi   have done
Oblique—
d) Conditional...........su-bekarazareba.........as, or since (I, etc.) should
                                             etc., not do
e) Hypothetical..........su-bekarazu(m)ba........if (I, etc.) should. etc., not
                                             do
f) Actual Concessive......su-bekarazaredomo......though (I, etc.) should
                     su-bekarazu to iedomo   etc., not do
g) Hypothetical Concessive su-bekarazaru mo........even if (I, etc.) should, etc.
                                             not do

PROHIBITIVE FORMS

Indicative—
h) Indefinite Form........su-majiku
i) Present: Conclusive....su-maji
   Attributive........su-majiki   Same renderings as for
j) Past: Conclusive......su-majikariki   corresponding Potential
   Attributive........su-majikarishi   Forms
Oblique—
k) Conditional...........su-majikereba
l) Hypothetical..........su-majiku(m)ba
m) Concessive...........su-majikeredomo

ILLATIVE FORMS

Indicative—
n) Past: Conclusive......sezari-keri..............(I, etc.) did not do. have,
   Attributive........sezari-keru   or had not done
Oblique—
o) Conditional...........sezari-kereba...........as, since, or when (I, etc.)
                                             did not do, have, or had
                                             not done
p) Concessive...........sezari-keredomo.........though (I, etc.) did not do.
                                             have, or had not done

---

q) Passive Form.........seraruru or saruru (§§ 193, 194)
   Causative Form......seshimuru or sasuru (§§ 126, 199, 200)
   Passive Causative Form seshimeraruru (§§ 130, 201, 221b)

REMARKS ON THE CONJUGATIONS
INFINITIVE

150. Japanese verbs have no infinitive properly so called. The present tense and such expressions as **yuku koto,** "the act of going," **yukishi koto,** "the act of having gone," supply its absence.

INDEFINITE AND GERUND

151. The use of the indefinite forms is explained in § 109. In the negative voice the gerund supplies the absence of an indefinite form (§ 120*l*).

INDICATIVE AND OBLIQUE MOOD

152. The fundamental distinction between the indicative and the oblique moods is that each tense of the indicative contains a conclusive form which is used to terminate sentences, and an attributive form which is used like an adjective prefixed to nouns (§§ 110 and 111), whereas no oblique mood can end a sentence, or be prefixed to a noun. In fact the oblique moods are verbs pure and simple, whereas the tenses of the indicative moods are of the nature of the participles. The gerund, like the oblique moods, is verbal only.

PRESENT TENSE

153. The Japanese use the present tense more commonly than we do. Not only do they employ it for general assertions, but they frequently denote by it past events, unless the fact of such events being past is the most noteworthy thing about them. Future events are also sometimes indicated by the present tense, if there is no doubt as to the certainty of their occurrence.

PAST TENSE

154. The *first past* is the original and true past tense, expressing, as it does, past time and nothing more.

155. The other pasts, when analyzed, are found to be compounds formed by means of auxiliary verbs, a trace of whose proper signification still survives. Thus **yukitari** is for **yukite ari,**

lit., "is having gone." **Yukitariki** is the same as **yukitari** with
the sign of the first past tense added.   Both of these are generally
best rendered by the English perfect, but sometimes by the
present, thus: **Chichi ni nitari,** "He is like his father."

156. Do not confound it with **tari, taru, tareba,** etc., contractions of **to ari, to aru, to areba,** etc., suffixed to nouns.   The most
literal rendering of these latter forms is the verb "to be," but
they are often best omitted from an English translation; thus:
giin taran mono, "those who may constitute (lit., 'be') the as-
sembly," i.e., "the members in the future."

157. **Inu** and **inuru,** the terminations of the fourth past, are
themselves the present of an old verb signifying "to go away."
The use of the fourth past therefore indicates that the action of
the verb is completely finished and done with.   Thus **suginuru**
means "It has passed away."   The only verbs of the fourth
conjugation which possess the fourth past are **kiru,** "to wear,"
niru, "to boil," and **niru,** "to resemble."

158. Some verbs form the fourth past by means of the
terminations **nu** and **nuru;** others by means of **tsu** and **tsuru,**
as will be seen by reference to the conjugations.   A few verbs
take either set of terminations indifferently; thus: **homenuru**
or **hometsuru,** "(I) have praised."   The fourth past is now
seldom seen.

159. Do not confound **nu,** the conclusive termination of the
fourth past, with **nu,** the attributive termination of the negative
present.   The one being conclusive and the other attributive,
they can never occupy the same place in the sentence.   In the
first conjugation, the two are further distinguished by the preceding vowel, which is **i** in the fourth past and **a** in the negative,
thus: **yukinu,** "went away," **yukanu,** "do not go."

PERFECT TENSE

160. The **perfect,** which exists only in verbs of the first conjugation and in the irregular verb **suru,** "to do," replaces the past,

and sometimes the present, when the action mentioned is a specific one.

FUTURE TENSE

161. The so-called future indicates not so much futurity as uncertainty, and may therefore be used in speaking even of present or past events if they are doubtful; thus: **Jū-hakku-nen mae no koto naran,** "It must have been some eighteen or nineteen years ago."

CONDITIONAL AND HYPOTHETICAL MOODS

162. The conditional and hypothetical, which are confounded together in the modern colloquial dialect of Tokyo, are sharply distinguished in the written language. Thus the conditional phrase **Karada sukoyaka nareba, yō ni teki su-beshi** means "As he is robust, he will do for the work," whereas the hypothetical **Karada sukoyaka naraba yō ni teki su beshi** means "If he is robust, he will do for the work." The hypothetical mood is sometimes emphasized by the use of the word **moshi,** "if perchance," placed at the beginning of the clause. The conditional followed by **nari** means "it is because." Thus: **Yō ni teki su-beshi, nan to nareba, karada sukoyaka nareba nari,** "He will do for the work (why, it is) because he is robust."

CONCESSIVE MOOD

163. The concessive mood is sometimes emphasized by the use of the word **tatoi,** "even though," at the beginning of the clause. In this case the clause usually ends in **to iedomo** or some contraction of it as **domo** or **tomo.** Occasionally the concessive words **to iedomo** are used in the sense of "even if," "even in"; thus: **Gunjin to iedomo bungaku no hitsuyo ari,** "Even if a soldier, literature is a necessity for him."

POTENTIAL AND PROHIBITIVE MOODS

164. The potential and prohibitive forms commonly replace the future and the imperative; thus: **yuku-beshi,** "I will go," rather than **yukan; yuku-bekarazu,** "you must not go," rather than **yukazare,** "go not"; **yuku-maji** rather than **yukazaran,** "I will not go."

DESIDERATIVE

165. The desiderative forms are used in two slightly different ways. Thus, while **yuki-taku** means "I want to go," **on ide nasaretaku** means "I want you to go." When suffixed to an honorific verb, the termination **taku** always refers to the writer, while the verb itself refers to the person addressed. When suffixed to a humble verb, the entire compound refers to the writer. In other cases a glance at the context generally shows whether **taku** should be referred to the subject or to the object. Thus: **Go rairin kore aritaku machi-tatematsuri-soro,** "I am waiting respectfully, wishing for your august approach," **i.e.,** "I hope you will come."

ILLATIVE

166. The illative tenses have been so designated because their distinctive termination **keri** was originally the perfect of the irregular verb **kuru,** "to come." In its original sense it means "it came to pass that" or "at length" as: **Hana wa saki keri,** "The flowers have at length opened." As shown in the conjugations, **keri** is agglutinated with the main verb; as **mi-keri** (§ 142*n*) which literally means "I have come having seen" and corresponds to the colloquial **mite kimashita.** Sometimes the main verb is followed by **te** or **ni** and then **keri,** as **aki wa ki-ni-keri,** "Autumn has come." The forms in **keri** may practically be considered to be equivalents of the first past, past conditional, and past concessive respectively. These forms are seldom met with except in classical writings.

UNUSUAL VERBAL FORMS

Besides the more usual verbal forms given in the conjugations there may sometimes be met with:

167. Archaic verbal forms in **aku,** which are used to introduce quotations. Thus: **iwaku,** "(he) says" (sometimes better rendered by "namely"), **ieraku**, "(he) said," both from **iu**, "to say"; **omoeraku**, "(I) thought," from **omou**, "to think." **Aku** indicates the present, **eraku** the past.

168. Futures formed by adding **ran** to the attributive present, as **aruran**, "shall be," **miruran**, "shall see."

169. A sort of periphrastic future denoting intention or being on the point of performing an action, formed by suffixing the words **to suru**, to the future proper; thus: **yukan to suru,** "to make to go," "to be on the point of going," "to be about to go"; **sen to suru,** "to be about to do." **Suru** thus used may be inflected through most of its tenses, as **yukan to seshi,** "was about to do," **yukan to shite,** "being about to do."

170. Forms indicating simultaneity, by means of **tsutsu** suffixed to the indefinite form, as **yukitsutsu,** "while going"; **mitsutsu,** "while looking."

171. Forms in **taran** derived from the second past, and nearly corresponding to the English future past, thus: **yukitaran,** "will probably have gone."

172. Such negative potential expressions as **yukazaru-beshi** for **yuku-bekarazu.** **Yukazaru-beshi** leans more to the sense of improbability or "may not go" than to the other senses of the potential.

173. Such expressions as **yukazumba aru-bekarazu,** "cannot but go," "must go," used to convey the sense of necessity.

IRREGULAR VERBS

174. Apparent irregularities are caused in large numbers of verbs by the inability of the Japanese to pronounce certain consonants before certain vowels and by the euphonic changes resulting from this inability. Thus from the stem **tat,** "to stand," we have **tatsu, tachi,** instead of **tatu, tati.** For a list of these important euphonic changes, see § 12.

175. Such verbs of the second conjugation as **kotayuru,** "to answer," mostly contract this attributive present into **kotōru** and conclusive present into **kotō.**

176. Verbs of the first conjugation whose stem ends in **s** such as **nokosu**, "to leave," **tsukawasu**, "to send," are sometimes conjugated in certain tenses as if they were compounds of the irregular verb **suru**, "to do." Thus we come across such forms as **nokoseshi** for **nokoshishi.**

177. Colloquial contractions, such as **atte** for **arite**, "being"; **kaute** or **kōte**, the Kyoto colloquial corruption of **kaite**, "buying," etc., are sometimes met with.

The only genuinely irregular verbs in modern written use are the following:

178. Aru, "to be," conclusive present, **ari** (identical with the indefinite form), instead of **aru.** No perfect tense. Otherwise conjugated regularly according to first conjugation with stem **ar.**

179. Keru, "to kick," conclusive and attributive present both **keru** (instead of **ku** and **kuru**, respectively). Inflections in **u** are replaced by inflections in **e** thus: conditional **kereba,** concessive **keredomo**, potential **ke-beku**, negative imperative **keru nakare.** Otherwise conjugated regularly according to second conjugation with the single letter **k** as its stem.

180. Kuru, "to come," conjugated according to third conjugation with stem **k**, except in the following tenses. Conclusive forms of first and second past not in use; future **kon**; present hypothetical not in use; optative **kobaya**; imperative not in use. Irregularities of negative voice: all the tenses down to first form of imperative have **o** instead of **i**, thus **kozu, kozaru, konu**, etc.; illative forms also have **o** for **i**, as **kozari-keri**, etc. **Kuru** is frequently supplanted by **kitaru**, properly the second past of **kuru**, but used as an independent verb of the first conjugation, and inflected regularly through all the moods and tenses, thus, **kitareri, kitariki, kitaritari**, etc.

181. Naru, "to be," indefinite form and gerund **nite**; present conclusive **nari** (instead of **naru**). No perfect tense. Otherwise conjugated regularly according to first conjugation from stem **nar.** Do not confound the irregular verb **naru**, "to be," with **naru**, "to become," which latter is a regular verb of the first conjugation. They are easily distinguished as **naru**, "to be," is never preceded by one or other of the postpositions **ni** and **to**, whereas **naru**, "to become," is always so preceded, thus: **Sakan naru machi**, "a prosperous town"; more lit., "a prospers town," i.e., "a town which prospers." (This is the attributive form of **naru**, "to be.") **Sakan ni naru machi**, "a town which is becoming prosperous" (attributive form of **naru**, "to become"). **Machi sakan nari**, "The town is prosperous" (conclusive form of **naru**, "to be"). **Machi sakan ni naru**, "The town is becoming prosperous" (conclusive form of **naru**, "to become").

182. **Neru**, "to sleep," conjugated similarly to **keru**, § 179.

183. **Shikaru**, "to be thus." Being a contraction of **shika aru**, it is conjugated like **aru**.

184. **Shinuru**, "to die," present attributive **shinuru** (for **shinu**). Otherwise conjugated regularly according to first conjugation with stem **shin**. It is not much used, the Chinese equivalent **shi suru** being preferred.

185. **Sōrō** (see chap. x).

186. **Suru**, "to do" (see complete conjugation of active voice beginning § 146). With the exception of its many irregularities it is conjugated according to the third conjugation. This is the most frequently used verb in the Japanese written language, for it is from the combination of this verb with nouns that most Japanese verbs are derived, as **kogeki-suru**, "to attack." It is seldom found alone with the meaning "to do." Note that where the preceding noun ends in **n** the **s** of the form of **suru** becomes **z** and **sh** becomes **s**. Thus **ronzuru**, "to discuss," indefinite **ronji**, conclusive present **ronzu**; perfect **ronzeri** and **ronzeru**, etc.

187. **Uru**, "to get" (colloquial **eru**). Its sole irregularity is that it has (in appearance at least) no stem, the real stem being the single letter which has vanished. It consists of the mere terminations of the second conjugation (§ 134), thus: indefinite

form **e**; present tense **u** and **uru**, etc.   It must not be confounded with **uru**, "to sell," which is a regular verb of the first conjugation.

188. **Uryōru**, "to grieve," indefinite form, **uree** or **urei**; attributive present, **uryōru**; conclusive present, **uryō**; potential tenses, **uryō-beku**, etc.   Otherwise it is conjugated regularly as a verb of the second conjugation from the stem **ure**.

PASSIVE AND POTENTIAL VERBS

189. The Japanese language has no special conjugation for the passive voice.   All so-called passive verbs are inflected according to the model beginning in § 122.   They are derived from the corresponding active verbs according to the following rule:

Insert between the stem and the inflections of the second conjugation:

CONJUGATION	INSERT
1	**ar**
2	**erar**
3	**irar**
4	**rar**

ACTIVE	PASSIVE
kiru, "to cut"	**kir-ar-uru**, "to be (more lit., 'to get') cut" or in its potential sense "to be able to cut"
matsu, "to wait"	**mat-ar-uru**, "to be waited for"
warau, "to laugh"	**wara-w-ar-uru**, "to be laughed at" (for the **w** see § 12*e*)

In the second, third, and fourth conjugations:

ACTIVE	PASSIVE
homuru, "to praise"	**hom-erar-uru**, "to be praised"
uramuru, "to hate"	**uram-irar-uru**, "to be hated"
miru, "to see"	**mi-rar-uru**, "to be seen"

The corresponding colloquial forms are **kirareru, matareru, warawareru**, etc.

190. The following passives (or potentials) in common use are formed irregularly:

> **koraruru** from **kuru,** "to come"
> **seraruru** (or **saruru**) from **suru,** "to do"
> **shinaruru** from **shinuru,** "to die"

Though formed irregularly from their stems, they are *conjugated* regularly, like all other passives and potentials, as verbs of the second conjugation.

191. A glance at the origin of the Japanese passive will furnish the student with a key to all the difficulties connected with it. Properly speaking, the so-called passive is not a passive at all, but simply an active in disguise. Such a form as **utaruru,** for instance, was originally **uchi ari uru,** as literally as possible "to get being beating," i.e., "to get a beating," or "to get beaten." Hence its place in the second active conjugation along with the verb **uru,** "to get," and hence the fact that intransitive verbs can have passive forms, as: **Ko ni shinaruru yori kanashiki wa nashi,** "There is nothing sadder than to have one's child die." (The Japanese idiom seems at first sight to be "to be *died* by one's child.") Hence, too, the frequent use of the postposition **wo** with these so-called passive verbs. Thus: **Teki ni danyaku wo torarete,** "their ammunition being taken by the enemy." More literally: "Having got their ammunition taken by the enemy." In this and all similar contexts where passive verbs are used, what is the subject of the true English passive is the object of the Japanese quasi-passive. The sentence may, or may not, have another subject expressed. Generally, as here, it has not, few Japanese sentences of any sort having subjects properly so called (see § 241).

192. The word "by" in English passive phrases is expressed in Japanese by **ni;** thus: **Inu ni ashi wo kamaruru,** "to be bitten in the leg by a dog," more literally, "to get one's leg bitten by a dog."

193. To the origin of the passive verb in an active form can likewise be traced the alternative use of the passive as a potential. Take, for instance, **miraruru,** lit., "to get a seeing." This form is naturally susceptible of two shades of meaning, which are either, "to get a seeing from someone else," i.e., "to get seen"; or, "to get a seeing one's self," i.e., "to be able to see." Similarly with **seraruru** the passive of the irregular verb **suru,** "to do." Signifying originally "to get a doing," it may mean either "to have something done to one," or "to be able to do."

194. From its use as a potential the use of the passive as an honorific is but a step, it being naturally considered more polite to intimate that an exalted personage *is able* to perform a certain action than bluntly to assert that he *does* it himself. This honorific use is the commonest use of the forms under consideration. Thus: **Waga seifu wa kanarazu Shina seifu ni tsuite kore wo yokyu seraruru** (for **suru**) **ni soi nashi,** "There is not the slightest doubt but that our government will demand this of the Chinese government."

195. Alternative methods of expressing potentiality are:

a) By prefixing the indefinite form, or suffixing the various inflected forms of **uru,** "to get," used in the sense "to be able." Thus: **e iwazu,** or **ii-ezu,** "I cannot say."

b) By using **uru** quite independently as: **Kanzezaru wo ezu,** "We cannot but feel astonished" (lit., "We do not get not wondering"), ... **yamu koto wo en ya,** "Can one help . . . . ?"

c) By suffixing the verb **atau,** "to be able," to the attributive present of other verbs to express potentiality; in its negative voice, to express impossibility, as **yuku atawazu,** "cannot go."

d) By suffixing the verb **kanuru,** "to be unable," to the indefinite form, to express impossibility, as **yuki-kanuru,** "cannot go."

CERTAIN INTRANSITIVE VERBS

196. There is a large class of verbs which it is generally convenient to translate by English passive or potential idioms, but which are properly intransitive in Japanese, and must be carefully distinguished from passives or potentials. Even in English, we feel a difference between two such assertions as "The gold is melting in the furnace" and "The gold is being melted in the furnace." In the first case, the action is represented as a spontaneous one; in the second case, it is explicitly the work of some outer agent. The verb of the former corresponds to the Japanese **tokuru,** "to melt" (intransitive); that of the latter to **tokaruru** (passive, "to get melted," derived from the transitive **toku,** "to melt")." Similarly the intransitives **miyuru,** "to be visible," and **odoroku,** "to start with fright," correspond very nearly, but not quite, to the passive-potentials **miraruru,** "to get seen" or "to be able to see," and **odorokasasuru,** "to get frightened (by someone)." Such intransitive verbs are never used honorifically.

TRANSITIVE AND INTRANSITIVE PAIRS OF VERBS

197. In English the same word commonly does duty both as a transitive and as an intransitive verb. Thus, "to melt," "to burn," "to stand," may be either transitive or intransitive according to the context. In Japanese the two meanings are expressed by different verbs derived from the same root, thus:

Intransitive

hiru (fourth conjugation), "to dry"
narabu (first conjugation), "to be in a row"
obiyuru (second conjugation), "to be frightened"
oruru (third conjugation), "to descend"
sadamaru (first conjugation), "to be fixed"
sazukaru (first conjugation), "to receive"
tatsu (first conjugation), "to stand"
ugoku (first conjugation), "to move"
yakuru (second conjugation), "to burn"
iru (second conjugation), "to enter"

Transitive

hosu (first conjugation), "to dry"
naraburu (second conjugation), "to put in a row"

[89]

> **obiyakasu** (first conjugation), "to frighten"
> **orosu** (first conjugation), "to lower"
> **sadamuru** (second conjugation), "to fix"
> **sazukaru** (second conjugation), "to give"
> **tatsuru** (second conjugation), "to set up"
> **ugokasu** (first conjugation), "to move"
> **yaku** (first conjugation), "to burn"
> **iruru** (first conjugation), "to put in"

198. The derivation of these pairs of verbs from the same root follows no fixed rule; but the stem of the transitive frequently ends in **s**. Many Japanese intransitive verbs must be translated by English reflexive verbs, as **asobu**, "to amuse one's self"; **ji satsu suru**, "to kill one's self"; **manzoku suru**, "to content one's self." The Japanese language has no reflexive verbs.

CAUSATIVE VERBS

199. Causative verbs are derived from transitive or intransitive verbs according to the following rule:

Insert between the stem and the inflections of the second conjugation:

CONJUGATION	INSERT
1	ashim
2	eshim
3	ishim
4	seshim

ACTIVE	CAUSATIVE
tsukur-u, "to make"	**tsukur-ashim-uru,** "to cause to make"
motom-uru (colloq. **motom-eru**), "to seek"	**motom-eshim-uru,** "to cause to seek"
ok-uru (colloq. **okiru**), "to get up, rise"	**ok-ishim-uru,** "to cause to get up, rise"
ki-ru, "to wear"	**ki-seshim-uru,** "to cause to wear"

200. There is an alternative way of forming the causative as follows:

Insert between the active stem and the inflections of the second conjugation:

CONJUGATION					INSERT
1	.	.	.	.	as
2	.	.	.	.	esas
3	.	.	.	.	isas
4	.	.	.	.	sas

Examples: **tsukur-as-uru, motom-esas-uru, ok-isas-uru, ki-sas-uru.**

201. All causatives are like other verbs, susceptible of the passive inflections, as **tsukur-ashim-erar-uru,** "to cause to make." This passive causative form, like all passive and causative forms, is conjugated as verbs of the second conjugation. The alternative forms as shown in § 200 are chiefly used, not as causatives proper, but as honorific substitutes for the simple intransitive or transitive verbs from which they are derived, e.g., **ar-as-erar-uru** for **aru,** "to be," **tazun-esas-erar-uru** for **tazunuru,** "to inquire," etc.

202. The causatives of **kuru, shinuru,** and **suru** are **kosashim-uru** (or **kosasuru**) **shinashimuru** (or **shinasuru**), and **seshimuru** (or **sasuru**) respectively.

203. Causative verbs are formed from adjectives by inserting **karashim** between the stem and the various inflections of the second conjugation, as **haya-karashim-uru,** "to cause to be early," from **hayaki,** "early."

204. Causatives are formed from negative verbs and adjectives by inserting **arashim** after the letter z in the termination of the present tense conclusive, as **motomez-arashim-uru,** "to cause not to seek," from **motomezu,** "(I) seek not"; **hayakaraz-arashim-uru,** "to cause not to be early," from **hayakarazu,** "not early." Such forms obtained from negatives as **motomez-arashim-uru,** "to cause not to seek," must be distinguished from the negative of the causative, as **motom-eshim-ezu,** "not to cause to seek."

205. There is also the form **motomez-arashim-erar-uru,** a passive causative negative, which can be used in an honorific sense, but is very seldom seen.

206. In causative constructions the name of the person who is made to perform the action is marked by the postposition **wo shite** (very rarely **ni shite** or **wo**); and the name of the person or thing the action is performed upon is marked by **wo.** Thus: **Hei wo shite kyōheki wo kizukashimu,** "He made the soldiers build a parapet." The passive converse of this would be: **Kyōheki wa hei no tame ni kizukashimeraru.** But such passive-causative constructions are scarcely ever used.

207. In general the Japanese are less scrupulous than we are in distinguishing the causative from the ordinary active idiom. Even in English, however, we often say that, for instance, we are building a house, when what we really mean is that we are having one built.

208. Notice, too, that the causative verb includes many shades of meaning. Thus **tsukurashimuru** must be rendered sometimes by "to cause to make," sometimes by "to allow to make" or "to let make." The fundamental idea of the causative is that, while the action is actually performed by one person, the question as to whether it shall be performed at all is in some way or other decided by another person. Sometimes the causation is a mere supposition, not real, thus: **Kono koto wo shite makoto nara-shimeba,** lit., "this thing if true (we) cause to be," i.e., "If we suppose this thing to be true."

209. Such transitive verbs as **obiyakasu,** "to frighten"; **tatsuru,** "to set up," etc., mentioned in § 297, must not be confounded with the corresponding and almost synonymous causative **obiyakashimuru,** "to cause to take fright"; **tatashimuru,** "to cause to stand up," etc. The transitives do not take the postposition **wo shite,** and are never used honorifically.

COMPOUND VERBS

210. Many complex assertions are made by means of compound verbs, which correspond either to the prepositional verbs of European languages or to whole phrases, thus:

mi-tōsu, "to look through," more lit.," to put through (by) seeing"
tsuki-tōsu, "to thrust through," more lit., "to put through (by) thrusting"
tsuki-korosu, "to thrust to death," more lit., "to kill (by) thrusting"
nige-saru, "to run away," more lit., "to depart (by) running"

As seen by these examples, the first verb is put in the indefinite form, and generally stands in an adverbial relation to the second, which alone is inflected. Very rarely the two are otherwise related, as **kai-modosu,** "to buy and give back," which has come to be used with the meaning "to buy back," "to repurchase"; **yuki-kaeru,** "to go and come back."

Some compound verbs consist of more than two members, as **tobi-agari-saru,** "to fly away in an upward direction."

ORNAMENTAL VERBS

211. Many verbs are used ornamentally, that is to say, without regard to their proper signification, and as mere embellishments of style. Thus **ai-sumu** and **makari-yuku** mean no more than the simple verbs, **sumu,** "to come to a conclusion," and **yuku,** "to go," the prefixes being meaningless in modern usage.

212. The verb **tamau,** properly "to give to an inferior," imparts an honorific tinge to the preceding verbs, thus: **mes-aserare-tamau,** for **mesu,** "to summon," used when speaking of the Emperor. (**Mes-as-erar-e** is the indefinite form of the potential of the causative of **mesu,** used honorifically.)

213. The verb **tatematsuru,** properly "to give to a superior," is used as a respectful suffix. **Negai age tatematsuri sōro,** "I most humbly request you. . . . ."

214. **Nari** (the conclusive present of **naru,** "to be") is the most usual ornamental verb, it being considered elegant to substitute for the conclusive forms of verbs and adjectives a periphrasis consisting of the corresponding attributive forms followed by **nari,** e.g.:

> **aru nari** for **ari**
> **bekarazaru nari** for **bekarazu**
> **naru nari** for **naru**
> **suru nari** for **su**
> **yoki nari** for **yoshi**

Shōkō wa heisotsu no mohan to iu beki nari, "Officers may be said to be models for the soldiers." (**Beki nari** is much more elegant than the plain conclusive **beshi** would be.) **Nari** is also often used after **sōrō** for ornamental purposes: **Moshi age sōrō nari,** "I have the honor to address you."

VERB "TO BE"

The following is a list of the Japanese verbs in modern written use corresponding to the English "to be":

215. **Aru** signifies "to be" when it forms part of an adjective, as **mezurashik-ariki,** "was strange"; **mezurashik-eredomo,** "though it is strange." The adjective proper and the verb **aru** are occasionally written separately, thus: **mezurashiku ariki, mezurashiku aredomo.** In almost all other cases **aru** corresponds to "there is," "there are," "there were," etc., thus: **Ni-shu ari,** "There are two kinds"—an assertion to be scrupulously distinguished from **Ni-shu nari,** "They are two (i.e., different) kinds." Similarly **arazu** (generally, however, replaced by the negative adjective **nashi**) signifies "there is not," while **narazu** signifies "(it) is not."

216. **Ar-as-erar-uru,** the potential-causative form of **aru,** is used honorifically for **aru,** when the actions of exalted personages are mentioned.

217. **Iru**, "to dwell," "to live," "to be" (in the sense of living), hence only used when speaking of living creatures, especially human beings. It may often be omitted when translating. Thus: **Yokohama ni iru gaikoku-jin**, "the foreigners (dwelling) in Yokohama."

218. **Naru** is the usual equivalent of the copula, "to be," thus **Hohei no buki wa ju nari**, "The arm of the infantry is the rifle." It is used to turn nouns into adjectives (§ 19c) and also very frequently as an "ornamental verb" (§ 214). Occasionally the circumlocution **ni aru** or **nite aru** is used instead of **naru**. Thus: **Toki imada kogeki no toki ni arazu** (instead of **narazu**), "It is not yet time for the attack." In such cases **ni** is not properly the postposition **ni**, but an old indefinite form of **naru**, "to be," now almost disused. **Nite** is the gerund of **naru**, "to be." In some cases **naru** stands for **ni** (the postposition "in") and **aru**, and must then be rendered by "in" or "at." Thus: **Nagoya naru** (for **ni aru**) **Dai Roku Rentai**, "The Sixth Regiment (which is) at Nagoya."

219. **Naku**, **nashi**, **naki** (sometimes called the "negative adjective") "there is not," "there was not," etc., thus: **Sōi nashi**, "There is no doubt."

220. **Oru** same as **iru**.

221. **Suru.** (*a*) Properly "to do," sometimes means "to be," as in **Oto suru**, "There is a noise"; **Ka to su**, "It is good." **Iu-beku shite, okonau-bekarazu**, lit., "being that one may talk, and that one may not do," i.e., "It may be talked of, but it cannot be done." **Yukazu shite** for **yukazu**, "(being) not going."

b) Often as in the last of these instances, it is most convenient to look on it as an expletive. **Nihonjin ni shite**, "being a Japanese."

c) Most frequently **suru** simply serves to verbalize nouns, as
    ai suru, "to love," from **ai**, "love"
    shi suru, "to die," from **shi**, "death"
    kaika suru, "to be civilized," from **kaika**, "civilization"

The resulting verb, as seen by these instances, is sometimes active, sometimes neuter, sometimes passive, usage alone deciding in each case which it shall be. To obtain an equivalent for the active verb, "to civilize," we must use the causative form **kaika seshimuru.**

d) **Suru** sometimes means "to be about to," as: **Sen to suru,** "I am about to do."

e) Sometimes it means "to consider," as: **Kinyō nari to suru,** "to consider important."

VERBS USED AS OTHER PARTS OF SPEECH

222. Some few verbs (mostly in the gerundial form) are used as postpositions. Thus (**ni**) **oite,** "in" (**oite** stands for **okite,** gerund of **oku,** "to place"); (**wo**) **motte,** "by means of" (**motte** stands for **mochite,** gerund of **motsu,** "to hold").

223. Others correspond to English adverbs, adverbial phrases, or conjunctions, thus:

hajimete, "for the first time," gerund of **hajimuru,** "to begin"
shiite, "urgently," "forcibly," gerund of **shiyuru,** "to press"
nokorazu, "without exception," "all," neg. gerund of **nokosu,** "to remain"
sareba, "that being so," "then," conditional of **saru,** "to be thus"
shibaraku shite, "after a little while," "shortly"
shikarazu shite, "on the contrary"

224. The attributive form of the present tense is sometimes doubled and used adverbially. Thus: **kaesu-gaesu,** "over and over again," from **kaesu,** "to turn over"; **miru-miru,** "before one's very eyes," from **miru,** "to see."

225. The attributive forms of verbs and adjectives, followed or not by **koto,** often correspond to English abstract nouns, or to English infinitives or present participles. Thus: **shimpo suru,** or **shimpo suru koto,** "progress," "to progress," "making progress," **naki koto,** or in the past tense **nakarishi koto,**

"absence." **Shimpo suru mono,** would mean "a thing (or person) that progresses"; **naki mono** "an absent thing" (or person). For though both **koto** and **mono** are most literally rendered by the English word "thing," **koto** always refers to abstract things, facts, affairs, matters, etc., while **mono** generally refers to actual tangible objects, and even to persons.

CHAPTER IX

THE EPISTOLARY STYLE

226. The epistolary style, as its name indicates, is that employed in letters and dispatches. Its use is not, however, limited to these. It is frequently met with in notices and advertisements, and occasionally in books and newspapers. In the latter it appears chiefly as a conventional substitute for the colloquial, that is to say, that it is used when it is desired to reproduce, as exactly as may be, the actual words spoken by some person quoted. To give these words in the colloquial would be considered an infringement of the dignity of written speech.

While this subject is handled here in a few pages, the art of actually reading letters written in the handwriting of the Japanese is a difficult study requiring years in which to become efficient.

227. The peculiarities distinguishing the epistolary style from the ordinary written style, treated of in the preceding pages, are very marked. These peculiarities are shown in their conjugation and phraseology.

A PECULIAR CONJUGATION OF VERBS AND ADJECTIVES

228. Almost every verb is turned into a compound by means of the irregular verb **sōrō,** which is suffixed to the indefinite form. Originally **sōrō** was an independent verb, **samurau,** signifying "to be in attendance on" (cf. **samurai,** "an attendant on a feudal lord"). When used alone it signifies nothing more than "to be." When added to other verbs and adjectives it is a meaningless suffix, generally corresponding to the **masu** of the colloquial. **Goza sōrō** is more honorific than **sōrō** alone. **Zonji sōrō** is the same as **omou,** "to think." The conjugation of **sōrō** is irregular and defective, the following being the only tenses in ordinary modern use:

> Present (also used for the past, and without any distinction of conclusive and attributive forms) .... sōro
> Future .... sōrawan
> Conditional .... sōraeba
> Hypothetical .... sōrawaba
> Actual Concessive .... sōraedomo
> Hypothetical Concessive .... sōrōte mo
> Gerund .... sōrōte

229. Sōrō having no indefinite form, the indefinite form of the plain verb is used instead to mark the end of a subordinate clause. The gerund or the indefinite form of the plain verb is also generally preferred to the gerund sōrōte. The future sōrawan is rare, being almost always replaced by the (properly potential) termination **beku sōrō**. The conditional sōraeba is not infrequently used for the hypothetical sōrawaba. In the negative voice sōrō is suffixed to the gerund of the plain verb. In adjectives it is suffixed to the indefinite form.

230. The ordinary conjugation of a verb in the epistolary style is therefore as follows:

EPISTOLARY CONJUGATION

itasu, "to do" (stem itas)

AFFIRMATIVE VOICE

Indefinite Form .... itashi
Present or Past .... itashi-sōrō .... (I) do, or did
Future or Potential .... itasu-beku sōrō .... (I) shall do
Conditional .... itashi-sōraeba .... as (I) do
Hypothetical .... itashi-sōrawaba .... if (I) do
Actual Concessive .... itashi-sōraedomo .... though (I) actually do
Hypothetical Concessive ... itashi-sōrōte mo .... even if I do
Gerund .... itashite .... having done, doing
Desiderative .... itashi-taku sōrō .... (I) want to do

NEGATIVE VOICE

Indefinite Form......... } itasazu.................not doing, not having done
Gerund................. }
Present or Past...........itasazu sōrō.............(I) do not do
Future.................itasu-majiku sōrō.......(I) shall not do
Conditional..............itasazu-sōraeba..........as (I) do not do
Hypothetical.............itasazu-sōrawaba.........if (I) do not do
Actual Concessive........itasazu-sōraedomo........though (I) do not do
Hypothetical Concessive...itasazu sōrōte mo........even if I do not do

231. Of the conjugation of adjectives, the following examples
may suffice:

Present: **yoroshiku sōrō,** "(it) is good"
Concessive: **yoroshiku sōraedomo,** "though (it) is good"

232. Sōrō is often dropped after adjectives, especially after
taku and **beku.** Thus: **Shōsei shuttatsu mae baikyaku itashi-
taku (sōrō) ni tsuki,** "as I am desirous of selling it before my
departure." Comprehension of such constructions, which are
common in the epistolary style, will be facilitated by noting
that, in the case of an honorific verb with the desiderative termination **taku,** the verb itself always refers to the honored person and
the termination to the writer. Thus: **On ide kudasare-taku-
sōrō** means lit., "(I) am wishing (you will) condescend august
coming," i.e., "I hope you will come."

233. The Chinese nouns, which are verbalized by means of
suru in the ordinary style of books and newspapers, are in the
epistolary style mostly verbalized by means of **itashi-sōrō,** or
of the more polite **tsukamatsuri-sōrō** for the first person, and
kudasare-sōrō or **nasare-sōrō** for the second. Thus: **Tōchaku
itashi-sōrō,** or **tōchaku tsukamatsuri-sōrō,** "I (or some other
humble person) have arrived"; **Go tōchaku asobasare sōrō,** "You
(or some other honorable person) have arrived."

234. Sometimes **sōrō** is suffixed directly to nouns, without the
intervention of **itasu** or **suru,** as **Kikan haidoku (itashi** or
tsukamatsuri) sōrō, "I have had the honor to peruse your letter."

A PECULIAR PHRASEOLOGY

235. Besides its actual conjugational forms, **sōrō** combines with a number of nouns to form peculiar idioms. Politeness also requires the constant repetition of honorifics and of ornamental verbs.

Sōrō aida, "because I do" or "I do . . . . and so"
Sōrō dan or **sōrō jō,** "inasmuch as," "and therefore," "and"
Sōrō ni tsuki, "owing to"
Koko ni makari ari sōrō tokoro, "while (I) was here"

236. Letters always open with some such polite phrase as **haikei,** "I beg to state"; or, in replies, **On tegami rakushu tsukamatsuri-sōrō,** "Your honorable letter is to hand"; **kikan haiken (tsukamatsuri-sōrō),** "I have seen your flowery epistle"; etc. Then (at least in private letters) comes a sentence in which the correspondent is congratulated on the good health which he enjoys notwithstanding the adverse state of the weather—this, despite the fact that the writer probably has no information on the subject. Thus: **Reiki ai-tsunori-sōrō tokoro, masu-masu go seifuku keiga tatematsuri sōrō,** "I beg to congratulate you on the perfect way in which you keep your health, notwithstanding the increasing coldness of the season." The real subject of the letter is then introduced by the words **nobureba** or **shikareba.** Sometimes, especially in postcards, the introductory compliments are superseded by some such apologetic phrase as **Zenryaku; go kaiyō kudasaru-beku sōrō,** "I omit compliments; pray excuse me for so doing." Letters are closed by some such phrase as **Kono dan kii e-taku,** or **Migi mōshi-age-taku, kaku no gotoku ni goza-sōrō nari,** "I beg to bring the foregoing to your favorable notice"; **On kotae katagata kii e-sōrō,** "I take the occasion of this reply to bring the foregoing to your favorable notice." To these some such expression as **tonshu,** "I bow my head," **sō-sō,** "hastily written," **fugu,** "insufficient," **Keigu,** "respectfully," is usually added.

237. In official dispatches, the introductory phrases, down to **shikareba** or **nobureba** inclusive, may be freely rendered by "I have the honor to inform you that . . . . ," or, in the case of answers, by "I have the honor to acknowledge the receipt of your communication of the . . . . instant, and to state in reply that. . . . ." Such English paraphrases of the opening words may also be held to include the resumptive final phrase **Kono dan kii e-taku,** while **tonshu,** etc., may be paraphrased by "I have the honor to be, etc." With obvious slight changes, the same remarks apply to the translation of private letters.

238. Some of the difficulties of parsing, which are specially prominent in the epistolary style, will be found discussed in § 244.

239. The epistolary style has here been discussed very briefly. A separate textbook could well be written on this subject alone.

CHAPTER X

SYNTAX

240. The fundamental rule of Japanese construction is that qualifying words precede the words they qualify. Thus the adjective or genitive precedes the noun which it defines, the adverb precedes the verb, and explanatory clauses precede the principal clause. The object likewise precedes the verb. The verb (or predicative adjective) of each clause is placed at the end of that clause, the chief verb (or predicative adjective) rounding off the entire sentence.

By an exception, which is merely apparent, postpositions follow, instead of preceding, the words which they define. Similarly, the interrogative particles follow the words whose sense they modify.

As an example of this first rule, we have: **Sakujitsu uketori-taru tegami,** "Yesterday received letters"; **Muyō no mono iru-bekarazu,** lit., "No business persons enter may not," i.e., "No admittance except on business." (**Mono** is the subject, defined by **muyō,** which accordingly precedes.)

241. Most sentences are subjectless, the verb expressing rather a coming to be with reference to some person than an act explicitly declared to be performed by him. Should there be a subject, it is generally placed at the head of the sentence. More frequently the word which it is wished to lay stress on is isolated by **wa** and heads the sentence.

Taikyaku seba fuka naru-beshi to omoite, tsui ni sono mei ni shitagau, "(He) ended by obeying the command thinking that it would be improper for (him) to retreat"; or lit., "If retreat improper will-be-thinking-that (he) at last that command obeys" (**shitagau,** historic present, instead of past **shitagaiki,** "obeyed").

As here shown the clauses forming a Japanese sentence must often be translated in inverse order, English construction generally preferring to place the chief statement first, and the explanatory phrases after it.

242. The predicative verb or adjective of the final clause of a sentence is put in the conclusive form (subject to a few exceptions caused by the presence of interrogative words and of certain particles or postpositions, see **zo,** § 64), while the predicative verbs or adjectives of all the preceding clause meant to express the same tense or mood as the verb of the final clause are put in the indefinite form. Similarly in the case of a set of clauses having an attributive, conditional, hypothetical, or gerundial signification, it is only the verb of the last clause of the set that appears in the attributive, conditional, hypothetical, or gerundial form, all the preceding verbs being put in the indefinite form.

Keirō wo hogeki shi, Fukushū wo arashi, Tansui wo seme, Neiha wo osoi, Tonkin no sakai wo koete, Kōsei ni seme iri, higō no shōri wo u, "Having bombarded Keelung, ravaged Foochow, invested Tamsui, attacked Ningpo, and crossed the frontiers of Tonquin, (the French) pressed forward into Kwangsi, and gained a very great victory."

Here the indefinite verbal forms of the first four clauses, viz., **shi, arashi, seme,** and **osoi,** having the meaning of gerunds, because the fifth verb **koete** is a gerund; the indefinite verb **seme-iri** has the meaning of a present indicative (historical present used for the past), because the final verb **u** is in the ordinary conclusive form.

243. The difficulty of finding a subject may frequently be eluded by substituting an English passive for the Japanese active construction, as the version can then be vague without ceasing to be grammatical. For example: **Sude ni fukoku seshi tōri,** "as has already been notified" (the Japanese verb, though active, does not state by whom). At other times the translator must invent a subject appropriate to the context, such as "it," "they," "the persons in charge," "the government," etc.

244. Note also such constructions as the following which cannot be parsed at all according to European rules: **Hito no kokoro no shirigataki, katachi wo motte sadamuru koto kanau-bekarazu,** lit., "The difficulty of knowing the hearts of men— settling (it) by means of faces will not suit," i.e., "The difficulty of knowing the hearts of men cannot be solved by an appeal to their faces."

Or the following taken from the bulletin board of a steamer: **Go shoji no shina banji go yōjin araserare-taku sōrō,** "Passengers are requested to be careful of their effects," lit., "Articles of august possession, everything are wanting to be able to cause to be august care." Here the verb **aru** belongs to **yōjin** "care"; the causative-potential termination **aserare,** honorifically used, indicates respect toward the passengers, who, however, are not explicitly mentioned; **taku** refers to the managers of the steamship company, also not mentioned, and **sōrō** is a mere ornamental suffix **(taku, § 232).**

245. Another common construction violating European rules is that in which a quotation is both prefaced and rounded off by some verb meaning "to say," thus: **Iwaku ". . . ." to,** i.e., "He said: '. . . .' was what he said." To make sense in English, we must suppress either the first "said" or the second.

246. After what has been said in § 60, the student should not fall into the error of taking the postposition **wa** in the two succeeding examples for a sign of the nominative case. **Jōtō wa ichi-en, katō wa go-jis-sen nari,** "The first class is a dollar, and the second fifty cents," lit., "As for the first class (it) is a dollar; as for the second, fifty cents." **Seito wa gakushi to shite maigetsu kin shichi-en wo osameshimu,** "The pupils are to pay seven dollars a month as school-fees," lit., "As for the pupils (the authorities) cause (them) to pay every month seven dollars money as school-fees."

247. Negatives destroy each other, as in English, thus: **Kimyō
to iwazaru bekarazu,** "(We) cannot but call it strange." **Kore
wo shirazumba-aru-bekarazu,** "(One) must not fail to know this."

248. Japanese has no negative pronouns or adverbs like the
English words, "none," "neither," "never." Their absence is
supplied by the negative forms of the verb, combined with
positive pronouns and adverbs. Thus, for the English "I know
nothing," a Japanese will write **Nani mo shirazu,** "I know-not
everything."

249. The following examples will show how the various kinds
of English negative or quasi-negative assertions are expressed
in Japanese:

Kitaru koto nashi, or **Hito-tabi mo kitarazu,** "He never
comes." The first form means literally "coming thing is **not**";
the second is "even once comes not."

Kitaru toki mo ari, or **Kitaru koto mo ari,** "He sometimes
comes"; more lit., "There are also times when (he) comes";
"There is also such a thing as (his) coming."

Kitarazaru toki mo ari, or **Kitarazaru koto mo ari,** "He sometimes does not come," i.e., "He does not always come."

Mattaku shirazu, "I do not know at all," lit., "Quite know
not."

Kuwashiku wa shirazu, "I do not quite know," lit., "as for
minutely, (I) know not."

Shito hito nashi, "No one knows," lit., "There is not a knowing person."

250. The difficulty of using negative construction correctly
will disappear, if it is borne in mind that in Japanese the negative
and the verb are not conceived of as two separate ideas, as is
mostly the case in English, but as a single idea. Even in English,
however, there are plenty of parallels to this Japanese idiom.
Thus, "incapable" for "not capable," "to dislike" for "not to
like," "difficult" for "not easy." If, for instance, instead of
rendering **mattaku shirazu** by "I do not know at all," we render

it by "I am entirely **unaware**," the Japanese construction ceases to appear abnormal.

251. Occasionally a negative is limited by suffixing **wa** or **shi mo** (shi is a meaningless expletive); thus: **Kanarazu kitarazu,** "He certainly will not come"; but **Kanarazu shi mo kitarazu,** "He is not certain to come."

252. Interrogation is marked, not as in English by an inversion of the construction, but by the use of interrogative particles (see **ka,** § 55, and **ya,** § 62). Note that the conclusive form of the verb is, in interrogative sentences, generally changed to the attributive form.

253. In a rhetorical question, where a negative reply is expected, the word **ani** is placed at the beginning of the sentence, and **ya** at the end, thus: **Ani hakaran ya,** "Would anyone suppose so?" (i.e., "Of course no one would have supposed so").

254. The scanty use of subjects and more especially of pronouns with the verb, and the absence of persons in the verb, are made good to some extent by an abundance of humble and honorific expressions, thus:

      settaku, "my house," lit., "the awkward house"
      heisha, "our firm," lit., "the broken firm"
      on taku, "your house, lit., "the honorable house"
      kisha, "your firm," lit., "the exalted firm"

255. In many cases different words are chosen, according as low-class persons (e.g., myself) or high-class persons (e.g., you) are spoken of. Thus while **yuku** is the plain verb meaning "to go," it is polite when writing of one's self to use the respectful synonym **mairu,** or some such circumlocution as **sanjō tsukamatsuru** (lit., "to go respectfully to the abode"); when writing of the person addressed we use **on ide nasaru** (lit., "to be able to do an august outing"); when referring to the Emperor we use **araseraruru** (lit., "to be able to cause to be able"). The honorific use of passive and causative verbs is particularly frequent (see §§ 194 and 201).

256. In Japanese all quotations, whether of one's own thoughts or of the words of others, are direct. The many changes of person and tense which are caused in English by the use of indirect quotation are consequently unknown. A Japanese does not say, "They promised that they would come." He says, "They promised that 'we will come,'" **Ware-ra kitaran to yaku-soku seri,** thus repeating the actual words used by the speakers quoted. Quotation is marked by suffixing the postposition **to,** "that," or **tote** and occasionally by prefixing some such expression as **omoeraku,** "I thought," **ii-keru wa,** "as for what he said (it was). . . . ."

257. Verbs are sometimes omitted at the end of a sentence, especially in the higher Chinese style. The omission of the verb, generally speaking, adds force to the statement. The verb must be supplied from the context, thus: **Tōbun no uchi kyugyō (su),** "Closed for the present."

258. After the word **nomi,** "only," the final verb **nari** is generally thus omitted, as: **Nani no nasu beki hōhō naku teishi suru nomi (nari),** "It cannot be helped, and all (they) can do is to halt," more lit., "There is not any way that one may do (and it is) only halting."

259. Passive constructions are very rarely used. They are almost always replaced by the subjectless active constructions explained in § 243. The grammar of the passive is peculiar (see § 191).

260. Inanimate objects are rarely, if ever, personified. It is hardly permissible even to use the name of an inanimate object as subject of an active verb. Thus a Japanese will not say or write, "The rain delayed me," but "I have become late on account of the rain," **Ame no tame ni chikoku seri.**

261. Languages differ greatly in the degree of integration of their sentences. Thus, Chinese and Pidjin English simply put assertions side by side, like stones without cement, as "He bad man. My no like he." Our more synthetic English would generally subordinate one of such a couple of assertions to the other, as "I don't like him, because he is a bad man." Now one of the most essential characteristics of the Japanese language is the extreme degree to which it pushes the synthetic tendency in the structure of sentences. Except when modified by Chinese or other foreign influence, Japanese always tries to incorporate the whole of a statement, however complex it may be, and however numerous its parts, within the limits of a single sentence, whose members are all grammatically interdependent. In fact, the normal Japanese sentence is a paragraph, or (so to say) an organism, as much more complicated than the typical English sentence just quoted as the English sentence is more complicated than the Chinese or Pidjin English. For this reason it is difficult to translate literally into English, so as to convey the true meaning.

262. Grammatical interdependence between clauses is secured chiefly as shown in § 242, by the incorporation of quotations, by the use of the conditional and concessive moods, and by the use of the corresponding particles **ga, ni,** and **wo** suffixed to verbs. In translating a Japanese sentence into idiomatic English, it is generally necessary to break it at several of these hinges, as they may perhaps be termed.

CHAPTER XI

DETERMINATION OF THE MOOD AND TENSE

263. To the beginner in the study of the written language, it is most important that he be able to determine promptly what the mood and tense of the verb or adjective as shown by its inflection signifies. Many of us have struggled through several years of study of this language without securing a clear idea of these inflections. It is my hope here to show the student or translator a method by which he can quickly understand the particular verb or adjective as he encounters it in his reading.

264. To be able to translate a Japanese sentence, we must understand the construction of the sentence. To understand the construction of the sentence, we must understand the verbs and their relation to each other. To understand a particular verb, we must know its mood, tense, and form.

265. To determine its mood, tense, and form, we must first determine its **romaji** stem and its **romaji** inflection. Looking up the inflected part in the alphabetically arranged *list of inflections*, we have a number referring us to a section where we find the translation of a verb or adjective similar in form to it.

266. The general rule for determining the stem and inflection of the verb is: *the* **romaji** *stem consists of the character plus the consonant of the following* **kana;** *the remainder constitutes the inflection.* For example, let us take the verb **uritari** (verb "to sell"). Here the character is read **u,** the first syllable of the **kana** inflection is **ri.** Applying the rule, we have **ur** for the stem and **itari** for the inflection. Looking in the alphabetically arranged list of inflections on page 130, we are referred to the first conjugation, indicative mood, second past, conclusive (§ 118*e*) and then from the context we must decide whether it is "sold," "have sold," or "had sold."

267. An exception to this rule is found in the fourth conjugation in which the character and the stem are the same, and the **kana** and the **romaji** inflection are the same; for example, the verb **miru**: here the stem is **mi** and the remainder **ru** the inflection. It is of interest to note that the stem in this case ends in a vowel. Fortunately there are very few of these verbs (list in § 123).

268. An apparent further exception to this rule is the irregular verb **suru** which is always written in **kana** only. However, it follows the rule and its stem is **s**.

269. But this general rule alone is not going to help the beginner until he has passed beyond the eighth **Tokuhon,** for in the sixth, seventh, and eighth **Tokuhons** we find the majority of the verbs written in **kana** only. To determine the stem in this case, it is necessary to look up the present conclusive form in Inouye's *Japanese-English Dictionary* or one similarly arranged, and there we find the verb written in characters and **kana,** from which by applying the rule we find the stem and the inflection.

270. The general rule for the verb cannot be applied to adjectives. They generally appear written, like verbs of the fourth conjugation—their stem in characters and inflection in **kana**; but there are some exceptions to this rule. Bear in mind that the adjectival inflection usually begins with **k** (§ 106).

271. As an aid to the memory we have the sign of the conjugation as in the following table:

	PASSIVE	CAUSATIVE		
First conjugation	**ar**	**ashim**	and	**as**
Second conjugation	**erar**	**eshim**		**esas**
Third conjugation	**irar**	**ishim**		**isas**
Fourth conjugation	**rar**	**seshim**		**sas**

	PASSIVE OR HONORIFIC	CAUSATIVE	
First conjugation	**ashimerar**	and	**aserar**
Second conjugation	**eshimerar**		**esaserar**
Third conjugation	**ishimerar**		**isaserar**
Fourth conjugation	**seshimerar**		**saserar**

272. There are two much used verbs which often are written in kana alone. The student should be able to recognize them at once and should remember their stems. They are:

>   **aru,** stem **ar,** first conjugation
>   **naru,** stem **nar,** first conjugation

273. Form the habit of using the index when desiring to understand some subject, word, or phrase.

ALPHABETICAL LIST OF INFLECTIONS OF THE VERB AND ADJECTIVE

* See also § 149q.

* See also § 200.

[115]

* See also § 200.

* See also § 200.

* See also § 137q.

* See also § 137*q.*

* See also § 137q.

[122]

* See also § 137q.

* See also § 137a.

[124]

* See also § 141q.

* See also § 141q.

* See also § 141q.

* See also § 141q.

ALPHABETICAL LIST OF INFLECTIONS

* See also § 141¶

[129]

ALPHABETICAL LIST OF INFLECTIONS

* See also § 145q.

* See also § 145q.

* See also § 1459.

* See also § 145q.

* See also § 145q.

[136]

ALPHABETICAL LIST OF INFLECTIONS

* See also § 145*q*

[137]

INDEX

INDEX

All references are to sections except as otherwise indicated. Japanese words are in boldface type.

INDEX

[143]

PRINTED IN THE U.S.A.